Charles X (m. Marie-Thérèse de Savoie)
King of France
1824–30

Duc d'Angoulême
(m. Marie-Thérèse-Charlotte,
daughter of Louis XVI)
1775–1844
Renounced his rights to throne in 1830
d. without posterity.

Duc de Berry
(m. Marie-Caroline de Naples)
1778–1820
he was murdered

Comte de Chambord
1820–83
(called Henri V)
d. without posterity

LETTERS FROM PARIS
1870 – 1875

The Boulevard des Italiens during the Second Empire

LETTERS FROM PARIS
1870–1875

Written by C. de B.
a political Informant to
the head of the London
House of Rothschild

Translated and edited by
ROBERT HENREY

LONDON: J. M. DENT & SONS LTD.

CONTENTS

ILLUSTRATIONS

1870–1941

In March 1941 a group of patriots defied death to circulate a typewritten newspaper called *Valmy* [1] in Nazi-occupied France. The editors quoted these lines from a speech made by Gambetta during the Franco-Prussian War:

No; it is impossible that the genius of France has been hidden for ever; that this great nation should allow her place in the world to be taken away because of an invasion of 500,000 men.

GAMBETTA.

[1] In 1792 the King of Prussia, watching the French Revolution, decided that it would be easy to beat the disorganized French army and steal some rich provinces. The Prussian troops poured over the frontier, but thousands of Frenchmen answered the call of 'The Nation is in danger!' and the Prussians were beaten at Valmy. That is why this newspaper, distributed in spite of the Nazis, bore this title.

I. INTRODUCING C. DE B.

FOR some thirty years following the return to France of Louis-Napoleon in 1848, the house of Rothschild in London received a daily news-letter from Paris on the trend of political events. This correspondence was not only kept up throughout the whole of the Second Empire, but was uninterrupted by the war of 1870, the Siege of Paris, and the Commune.

It continued thereafter until the country's vigorous recovery under the Third Republic.

The importance of these letters to future historians is immense. They may also throw some light on how France will make a similar recovery in the years to come.

The letters were addressed to Baron Lionel de Rothschild at New Court in St Swithin's Lane, E.C., by a Frenchman who signed himself with his initials, C. de B. Although time has allowed the writer to assume an incognito, a close study of his letters reveals occasional glimpses of his personality and of his private affairs.

He was a man of considerable wealth and political influence. We find him, during the presidency of Marshal MacMahon, giving orders to a group of newspapers under his control. He had close personal ties with several of the princes of the house of Orleans, but was equally at home with leading Republicans. Critical of the foreign policy of Napoleon III, he showed an unusually broad outlook.

This capacity for seeing things from a detached point of view makes his letters particularly valuable, but his most striking gift is one of clear thinking. He sums up a situation in a few lines and foretells the future with extraordinary accuracy.

Though C. de B. does not reveal the exact date of his birth, it must have been at about the time of Waterloo. His childhood was consequently spent under the reigns of Louis XVIII and Charles X, and his twenties during that of Louis-Philippe.

The letters are written in French, but not necessarily in the same hand, though always signed with his initials. In certain cases the correspondence was doubtless dictated to secretarial scribes, and one is also tempted to believe that he had a staff which functioned during short periods of his absence, because he paid visits to the various courts of Europe, notably to St Petersburg, without the correspondence from Paris being interrupted.

The letters I have chosen for this volume start with the outbreak of the Franco-Prussian War, and continue as a running narrative until the end of 1875, when France was on the eve of her stupendous recovery. Although, as I have pointed out, it is quite clear that C. de B. had instructions to write every day, there are gaps amongst the letters now in the archives at New Court. The only serious gaps in the four and a half years under review (1870–5) are in 1872. That is why I have placed in brackets a few notes of the main events of that year so that the reader may not lose the continuity of the story. These notes are mostly inspired by M. de Marcère's *L'Assemblée Nationale de 1871* (Paris, 1904–7), because M. de Marcère was himself a member of the National Assembly, and wrote, like C. de B., of what he saw and heard.

In spite of these gaps there are almost a thousand letters in the New Court archives written between July 1870 and December 1875. It would have been outside the scope of a volume like this one to give them in their entirety.

I have written an introduction in three chapters. The first, of which this is part, will remind readers of the chief events between the time Louis-Napoleon became emperor and the outbreak of the 1870 war. The second chapter of the introduction deals with a general review of events between the declaration of the war of 1870 and the end of the Siege of Paris, and the third chapter with events from the Commune to the confirmation of the Republic in 1875. Thus Chapters II and III cover the same period as the main letters which follow, my idea being to introduce the chief characters to the reader. Otherwise it would be particularly difficult, for instance, for anybody but an expert to understand the many intrigues for a restoration of the monarchy.

In looking carefully into the past in the hope of foreseeing the future we shall find similar mistakes, moments of muddling and despair. But these letters show the strength and resilience of France, and how it will rise again to new heights in spite of the errors of political and military leaders. One discovers daily doubts, hesitations, and hopes often forgotten or passed over in books written after the event. It is history told in slow motion.

C. de B. was a staunch patriot, whose political leanings appear to have been towards constitutional monarchy. Critical of Louis-Napoleon from the outset, there is a sharp tinge of irony in his long description of the emperor's marriage.

The first rumours of the betrothal are to be found in his letters of January 1853. Louis-Napoleon when younger had asked his cousin, the Princess Mathilde, to marry him. They were even engaged for a short time, but the engagement was broken off. Princess Mathilde was the daughter of ex-King Jerome of Westphalia, a younger brother of Napoleon I. At this period Princess Mathilde was married, but was living separated from her husband, Anatole Demidoff.

It was in her drawing-room, by one of those strange coincidences, that Louis-Napoleon met Mlle de Montijo, the daughter of a Spanish grandee. Paris was fully aware that Louis-Napoleon was captivated by her charm and youth, but Louis-Napoleon's supporters, while looking round for a bride, never gave a thought to Mlle de Montijo. They wished to consolidate the regime by a more brilliant marriage.

Here we have an example of Louis-Napoleon's strong will; he followed an idea with a dogged determination. While his followers were still searching for an ideal bride, Louis-Napoleon, quite unconcerned, invited Mlle de Montijo to every reception at the Élysée, as well as to all the hunting and shooting parties at Fontainebleau and at Compiègne, where she shone because of her beauty and remarkable horsemanship.

In December 1852, only a few days after he had become emperor, Louis-Napoleon invited several of his intimate friends to see the private apartments which he had just restored for his own use at the Tuileries. They were decorated with great luxury to celebrate the opening of the imperial reign. On reaching the room that was to serve as his study he took from his desk a garland of violets, which he placed on the head of Mlle de Montijo.

Shortly afterwards the emperor took up residence at Compiègne, where he had prepared entertainments on a lavish scale. Actors were brought from Paris, and plays were performed in the evening as in the days of the Bourbon kings. These spectacles were in honour of Mlle de Montijo and no secret was made of it, but nobody yet foretold marriage.

The suggestion was first taken seriously on 12th January. An imperial ball was held at the Tuileries, during which the Baron James de Rothschild, head of the Paris banking house, was seen to give his arm to Mlle de Montijo, whom he led to a sofa placed on the left of the imperial throne. As the young woman was about to take her seat, Mme Drouyn de Lhuys, wife of the Foreign Secretary, went over to her and whispered that the sofa was reserved for wives of Cabinet ministers. The young woman, blushing, murmured her excuses, and was moving away when the emperor, whose gaze never left her, advanced and led her to a seat on a sofa reserved for members of the imperial family.

Six days later C. de B. was sufficiently certain of the emperor's intentions to give definite news of the betrothal.

Both Napoleon's own family and his Cabinet were profoundly shocked by the engagement. King Jerome and his son, Prince Napoleon, received no official intimation from the emperor, and King Jerome did not leave his home for some days for fear of meeting his nephew and having to ask for an explanation. Princess Mathilde made an effort to dissuade her cousin from his coming marriage, but the only answer she received was an emphatic statement that Napoleon's decision was irrevocable. He added that he knew that the *salons* in Paris were not favourable to him, but said it was his belief that when the people of France saw a young and lovely empress at his side, they would applaud his marriage.

The fiercest opposition came from the Cabinet. Some ministers offered their resignations at the meeting presided over by the emperor, but when M. Fould was called on to speak the Finance Minister assumed the role of conciliator, hoping to make himself master of a delicate situation. M. de Persigny, Minister of the Interior, and M. de Saint-Arnaud continued in their objections, but the emperor announced curtly that the marriage was to be celebrated without delay, and that it was to take place at Notre-Dame.

The court needed a gilded coach for the marriage procession. C. de B. tells how one was found that had belonged to Louis-Philippe. When the arms of the ex-King of the French were removed, workmen discovered those of Charles X, and when these were removed, those of Louis XVIII. The coach that had served so many masters was given a new coat of paint, and Napoleon III ordered that on the day of the wedding it should be drawn by eight bays.

The public showed enormous interest in the coming marriage. But there was not any enthusiasm. Although Mlle de Montijo was of excellent family, she was not the princess that a whole nation loves to acclaim. The Cinderella in the gilded coach was a 'foreigner,' who brought nothing to France, neither a valuable alliance nor wealth.

The Government showed too much anxiety to organize demonstrations. The chief of police asked the women of the flower and vegetable markets to line the wedding route, and to carry bunches of violets. The corporations and guilds were told to bring out their banners and the workshops and dressmaking houses asked to see that their employees went out to cheer. Police inspectors called on the shopkeepers to urge them to illuminate their windows in the evening so as to add to the blaze of light from public buildings. The courtyard of the Louvre was garlanded with laurel leaves, but the cortège which was to leave the Élysée on the wedding day was suddenly cancelled, and the empress slipped away to the Tuileries by a back door in a closed carriage. When the procession finally left the Tuileries the weather, which earlier in the morning had been cloudy, turned bright.

I did not see a flag flying out of any window along the route, and the men did not uncover their heads as the imperial carriage passed. There was avid curiosity everywhere, for Parisians did not want to miss anything. The white plumes above the heads of the eight bays drawing the coach had immense success, and a wit shouted: 'It's just like a young girl's funeral procession!'

There was the same frigid atmosphere in Notre-Dame as amongst the public in the streets. When the emperor and the future empress entered the cathedral the members of the two Houses did not utter a single cry. The empress was very pale, but the emperor answered all the questions asked by the archbishop in a firm voice.   C. de B., 30th January 1853.

A round of balls followed the wedding, but Princess Mathilde, having with difficulty restrained her bitter feelings, showed a profound melancholy. This prevented her from attending the ball given by Mme de Persigny, at which the only member of the imperial family to be present was Prince Victor Napoleon.

Let us now briefly trace the historical events that led up to the Franco-German War.

On 23rd September 1862 Bismarck became Minister-President and Foreign Minister of Prussia. A German empire under Prussian hegemony was to be forged by his iron will. The fact that he was at first opposed to plans for German unification is immaterial. The policy was developed progressively, becoming apparent after 1866.

Now Napoleon III had been working on this idea for a considerable time. It was almost as much due to him as to Bismarck that a powerful and unified Germany arose. By the time Napoleon III realized where his dream was leading him, it was too late. He was mercilessly drawn into the war of 1870.

In 1850, when President of the Republic, Louis-Napoleon said to the Prussian Minister in Paris:

'Have not France and Prussia the same culture, the same ideals of enlightened liberalism, the same reasons to free and unite nations and races?'

Louis-Napoleon was then forty-two. He was still the obstinate dreamer of his youth, but it was not merely the unity of Germany that he desired. He dreamed of developing a spirit of nationalism everywhere, of assisting peoples of all countries to enfranchise themselves.

The deliverance of Italy haunted his imagination, but by this policy Austria must of necessity be weakened. Here again he was clearing, unconsciously, a way for Bismarck.

It was Napoleon I who, by a train of thought dictated to his aide-de-camp Las Cases at St Helena in 1816, first put the germ into his nephew's mind.

Las Cases, in his *Memorial of St Helena*, tells how on 11th November 1816:

'The emperor did not leave his room. I passed nearly all day with him, only leaving him to go and dine. The conversations of this day were long and full of interest, and his words were rich and rapid.'

After discussing a variety of subjects, the great Napoleon said to Las Cases:

'One of my most grandiose thoughts was the agglomeration, the concentration of peoples geographically the same who have been dispersed by revolutions or politics. Thus, in Europe there are, though not always together, thirty million Frenchmen, fifteen million Spaniards, fifteen million Italians, and thirty million Germans. I would have liked to make each of these peoples into a single nation. It is at the head of such a cortège that it would have been a fine thing to ride into posterity, blessed by centuries to come. I felt myself worthy of such glory!'

Napoleon I went on to picture a great European family under a system like the Greek Amphictyonic Leagues, with one set of laws, one set of moral principles. He pointed out that the unification of Italy was already far advanced, but that the German problem had not yet been solved. These are the words that his nephew pondered over:

'Why has no German prince ever weighed up the potentialties of his nation or known how to profit by them? If heaven had made me a German prince I would have undoubtedly governed all the thirty million Germans united. This unification will come sooner or later by the sheer force of circumstances. Since my overthrow and the disappearance of my system, I do not believe that European equilibrium is possible other than by the confederation of great nations.'

This argument ran directly counter to the traditional French policy laid down by Cardinal Richelieu, which was to abase Austria and at the same time to protect the many small German States. During the reign of Louis XV Choiseul pursued this policy, though he realized that the danger was no longer from Austria but from Prussia.

Napoleon I was a great enough man to break with this hitherto immutable law, but only because his personality and power dominated Europe. Even at St Helena, when drawing up a Europe of his dreams, he saw himself at the head of the cortège.

Napoleon III overlooked this important fact when he adopted his uncle's theories and tried to put them into practice.

Instead of working for the exclusive good of France, he worked for other countries. He was more the European than the Frenchman. He helped to unite and strengthen Germany, even taking Bismarck into his confidence for this great ideal when the 'good-natured ogre,' as he naïvely called the future chancellor, was accredited to the Tuileries in the summer of 1862. Bismarck flattered the emperor, though icily and with lofty condescension. When in September he was called back to Berlin to become Prime Minister he did not hesitate to pour scorn on the French court. 'I met two amusing women, not a single man.'

But Bismarck was not a European. He was solely and always a Prussian, which explains why he had no compunction in waging war against Napoleon III in 1870. Bismarck was not alone in being ungrateful. Napoleon III sacrificed his alliance with Britain to unite Italy for the crafty Cavour and Victor-Emmanuel, but he received no help from across the Alps when the German troops were converging on Paris. Crowds surged through the streets of Florence at the outbreak of the Franco-Prussian War shouting:

'Long live Rome and Prussia! Down with France!'

It was during the summer of 1858 that plans were drawn up for a united Italy. Cavour met Napoleon III at Plombières, and triumphantly carried back to Victor-Emmanuel a verbal understanding, or rather a promise to fight, that the King of Italy and his chief minister so ardently desired. France, in return, was to receive Nice and the Duchy of Savoy.

Queen Victoria, foreseeing that French intervention in Italy would probably lead France into war with Prussia, wrote to Napoleon III warning him that if he disturbed European peace he could no longer count on her friendship. But Napoleon did not listen. He made the first irreparable mistake of his reign— the abandonment of his alliance with Great Britain, which since the Crimean War had served him so well. He now left the bright years behind.

At the diplomatic reception in Paris on 1st January 1859,

Napoleon III approached the Austrian ambassador and, speaking slowly and emphatically, said:

'I am sorry that our relations are not so good as I could have wished, but please tell your emperor that my personal feelings for him are unchanged.'

In May he left Paris to assume supreme command of his army, which had preceded him into Italy. His troops were ill equipped; nothing had been prepared for the campaign. General Canrobert wrote (26th April):

'I have been given an army corps without staff officers, commissariat, ambulances, artillery, or sappers.'

To which Marshal Vaillant answered:

'I note with sorrow that your troops are not organized for war. You must do what you can.'

Magenta, the first victory against the Austrians, was announced to Napoleon III at dusk in San Martino just as he had lapsed into complete despair. In his relief he made MacMahon a Marshal of France; the victory of Solferino three weeks later earned a similar honour for Niel.

These two victories left Napoleon's army tired, grumbling, inadequately fed. Austria was still not decisively defeated, but Europe was becoming alarmed. The Czar Alexander dispatched his aide-de-camp, Shuvalov, to the Empress Eugénie at Paris to warn her. 'Make peace quickly or Prussia will attack France across the Rhine.' British public opinion was becoming hostile.

Napoleon III, disillusioned, rode along the dusty road to Villafranca to meet the young Emperor of Austria. The two monarchs complimented each other in a roadside cottage on their respective armies, and drew up an armistice which, for Napoleon, was almost a hasty compromise.

Back in Paris, Napoleon sought to explain this sudden caution:

'If I stopped the campaign it was not because my troops were worn out, or because of any abandonment of the noble cause I wished to serve, but because, in my heart, something spoke more earnestly still—the interests of France. . . .' As if to answer the obvious criticism that he might have consulted these interests earlier, the emperor went on: 'To help Italian independence I made war in defiance of the courts of Europe; as soon as danger menaced my country I made peace.'

The ground was now prepared for the first big testing of Bismarckian diplomacy. It took place in 1864.

The year opened gaily in Paris. French society was plunged into a round of entertainment. Though spurned by the monarchist aristocracy, the court of Napoleon III was the most picturesque and the most influential since that of Louis XVI. Apart from the splendour of the Tuileries, balls were held several times a week at the palatial homes of the dour Baron Haussmann, whom Napoleon had appointed Prefect of the Seine with dictatorial powers for the architectural replanning of Paris, and of Count Walewski, a natural son of Napoleon I.

Prussia now announced her intention of annexing the duchies of Schleswig-Holstein. The duchies were guaranteed by all the great powers, but the question was reopened in November 1863 by the death of Frederick VII, King of Denmark. This monarch was Duke of Schleswig and Duke of Holstein. While the new King Christian IX was being crowned at Copenhagen, Prussian intrigue attempted to draw the two duchies away from Denmark. The British Government watched the situation anxiously, and a word from Paris would have been enough to curb Bismarck. Both Napoleon III and his Foreign Minister Drouyn de Lhuys failed to realize the danger of abandoning their ally of Napoleonic days. Already troops from Saxony and Hanover occupied Holstein. Encouraged, Bismarck decided to indade Schleswig, whereupon Austria, anxious that Prussia should gain no undue advantage, announced her intention of acting in concert. On 1st February 1864 Austro-Prussian troops crossed into Denmark. Again Britain suggested united action with France. Napoleon III would not commit himself.

Thus he lost his first chance of checking Bismarck's policy of aggression before Prussia became too strong.

Lord Cowley called on Drouyn de Lhuys to insist on united Franco-British action against the German powers in virtue of the treaty of 1852. The Foreign Minister said that Napoleon believed that France had no major interests in the Danish affair, that the emperor's policy was favourable to the unification of peoples of kindred stock, and that he could not prevent the duchies from becoming German if this was their desire.

C. de B., 7th March 1864.

A conference took place in London. Each delegate had a map on which his Government had marked, according to its particular viewpoint, the new Danish frontier. As no settlement could be reached, the delegates played cards.

Bismarck saw that he could commit an act of violence and that France would not fight for her signature.

This was the supreme test of a policy of rapine that was to lead to the Seven Weeks War against Austria, and finally to 1870.

In July Napoleon III was at Vichy.

The emperor is continuing the same treatment as last year. He takes his bath at the thermal establishment at 6.30 every morning, but because he finds these baths too enervating, a bowl of sea-water salt is added, in spite of the advice of Dr Algerde, the establishment's medical adviser. During the day the emperor drinks at the 'Hospital' spring, and later goes for a walk. He shows much kindly interest in the Russian notabilities at Vichy, and invites many of them to his table. He seems very tired and worried, but is expected at the Château de Saint-Cloud on 3rd August.   C. de B., 18th July 1864.

The emperor is even more careful to avoid all political conversation at Vichy than at Fontainebleau, but on the rare occasions when he allows himself to speak he betrays strong displeasure at the turn of events in Dano-German affairs. He had hoped that the London conference would result in a rift between Britain and Germany, and even amongst the German States themselves. Nothing of the kind took place and Great Britain preferred a diplomatic failure to a quarrel with Germany. Napoleon also

*Queen Victoria welcoming Napoleon III and the Empress Eugénie
to Windsor*

hoped at one time that he would be chosen as umpire, and he showed hostility to Prussia when she refused a suggestion to this effect made by Great Britain. From the very beginning of the hostilities between Germany and Denmark Napoleon III wished to impose a plebiscite on the duchies.

All these things show how little the Napoleonic policy can congratulate itself on the results of the conflict, and the ill humour and presumption of the emperor are visible now that he realizes the present situation, which is graver for him than at any period during the last twelve years. The public has not yet realized the true position, and will only wake up to it when it is informed by events that will not be long in coming.

C. de B., 19th July 1864.

The emperor suffered an acute attack of his bladder trouble last week. He called his physician, Dr Larrey, at 6 a.m., and was obliged to stay in his apartment over the week-end. During the three days he remained in bed the emperor read the memoirs of Louis XIII, and on Sunday night, when an intimate friend called to see him, he laid down his book and exclaimed: 'Louis XIII was an absolute fool to let himself be ordered about by Richelieu. I shall never allow my ministers to obtain so much influence over me. They will always be the mere executors of my thoughts and my will.' C. de B., 30th August 1864.

For the Danish affair Austria had become Bismarck's ally. Bismarck was now planning to make her his victim. But he was not willing to embark on war until he was certain of its outcome. For this campaign he also needed the alliance of Italy and French support.

His task was not easy. Napoleon was wounded about the Danish affair, and had just ordered his ministers to send a confidential note to Paris and provincial newspaper editors ordering a more hostile tone towards Prussia. The note ended with these words, so prophetic that one wonders why the emperor did not act on them:

The Danish campaign has caused M. de Bismarck to lose his reason. He imagines himself to be the arbiter of Europe. His folly is not, however, without ability, and before he is cured a great deal of blood may be spilled.

C. de B., 25th August 1864.

Fourteen months later, in October 1865, Bismarck decided to visit Napoleon III. The emperor was beginning to seek in German affairs a definite solution of the Italian question. Bismarck intended to see how the land lay for an alliance.

The two men met first in Biarritz, and then in Paris, where the Minister of Finance was engaged in a major debate, in which he sought to cut thirty million francs from the army estimates.

On 3rd November Bismarck had an important meeting with the emperor. He exposed his favourite theories—how France had everything to gain from a larger and more powerful Prussia, how the small States not only constituted an obstacle to German reforms, but also were a direct menace to France.

Napoleon thought he was more than a match for the Prussian, but he was anxious about his public. Bismarck received no personal invitation to the Tuileries other than for political talks.

The Prussian minister showed some disappointment at not being invited to dinner by the emperor. On the day the big shoot took place at Ferrières at the Baron de Rothschild's, M. de Bismarck said he would not dine. He was expecting an invitation from Napoleon. When this invitation did not arrive he asked permission to remain for dinner at the château.

C. de B., 7th November 1865.

Though no formal treaty was arrived at during the visit, Napoleon promised to regard favourably an extension of Prussian power in Germany. He mentioned, however, that it was his personal desire to see Venice given back to Italy. Bismarck seized on this dream of Napoleon, for he foresaw the possibility of an Italian campaign against the southern armies of Austria while Prussia was attacking from the north. Before leaving Paris, Bismarck allowed Nigra, the Italian minister, to suggest an Italian alliance and common action against Austria, but he remained non-committal, answering that he was not fully authorized to commit the Prussian Cabinet on this matter. Later Bismarck remarked sardonically: 'If Italy did not exist, we should have to invent her.'

Thiers, ex-Premier of Louis-Philippe, who now returned to active politics after exhausting work on his *History of the Consulate and Empire*, foresaw the danger.

On 3rd May 1866 he made a remarkable speech, in which he predicted with fulminating clarity the unity of Germany under the Hohenzollerns. The warning was not heeded. Two months afterwards came news of the decisive battle of Sadowa. Austria, as Bismarck had planned, was caught and crushed between two fronts.

Many Frenchmen were alarmed. A Grand Council was held at Saint-Cloud, and a number of ministers, led by Drouyn de Lhuys, urged immediate intervention. There might still be time to prevent Prussia from becoming all-powerful. The Empress Eugénie, who now attended every Cabinet meeting, approved the views of Drouyn de Lhuys. Marshal Randon, Minister for War, questioned by the empress, said that he could send 80,000 men to Strasburg immediately and 250,000 more in twenty days. The emperor, white as a sheet, did not react. He was in ill health, disillusioned, at least temporarily, by his foreign policy, and was suddenly waking up to the fact that Sadowa, far from being a victory for France, as he had first thought, was a calamity.

The emperor listened in silence to Rouher and La Valette, the appeasers in his Cabinet, insisting on peace at any price; took no decision until the afternoon, when the Cabinet met for a second time, and the empress broke out again into a torrent of prophetic eloquence. Towards evening Napoleon made a vague promise to muster 50,000 men on the Rhine, but during the night, influenced by his cousin, Prince Napoleon, he changed his mind. In vain did the empress argue; Napoleon, caught up in something approaching fatalism, refused to intervene. Bismarck drew a long breath of relief. He was hardly able to believe in his good fortune, but immediately, with true Prussian harshness, he followed up his advantage. On 19th July, Goltz, Prussian minister in Paris, called on Drouyn de Lhuys to explain that Prussia now felt obliged, because of public opinion at home, to annex parts of Hesse, Saxony, and Hanover. Drouyn de Lhuys answered rather abruptly that he would speak to the emperor about it. Goltz left the Foreign Minister to his own reflections, and hurried to Saint-Cloud, where he asked for an interview with Napoleon III. The emperor showed so little opposition that Goltz was able to assure Bismarck that henceforth France would do nothing to stop Prussian expansion. 'Alas!' exclaimed Drouyn de Lhuys, when he learned of this. 'There is nothing left but to weep.'

Nevertheless Napoleon III demanded from Bismarck the left bank of the Rhine as far as Mainz as compensation for the Prussian territorial gains. Incidentally this demand was a violation of his sacred principle of concentration of like peoples. Bismarck refused, knowing that he was strong enough now to make no concessions, but as Napoleon put forward diminishing demands Prussia allowed them to linger in order to create suspicion of Napoleon's designs amongst the other powers. In the spring of 1867 Napoleon was merely claiming Luxemburg. By then he had lost so much prestige that Bismarck did not hesitate to speak with a sneer about France.

A Prussian diplomat employed by Bismarck for secret negotiations has reached Paris this morning. He says that the British Cabinet has very cleverly though quite unofficially intervened in the Luxemburg affair. The King of Prussia and Bismarck now appear willing to follow a path of conciliation with France in order to prevent war. It seems likely that some scheme will be found to neutralize the duchy and to demilitarize the fortress, which might remove any conflict between Prussia and France. C. de B., 20th April 1867.

The emperor appears much surprised and extremely annoyed at the lack of enthusiasm in France for a war against Prussia. In spite of the exhortations of the official press, another order had to be sent out to-day urging editors to redouble their zeal and whip up a martial feeling in the country.

At Saint-Cyr the young officer cadets in their first year are following second-year courses. People in Paris are sending their children and their aged parents to Normandy and to Brittany. Feverish activity is reported from Metz, where munition workers in cartridge factories continue working until midnight.

C. de B., 24th April 1867.

Three days later the fever abates.

The emperor is ready for war, but he is anxious to take full advantage of the success of the exhibition which is bringing to Paris so many crowned heads. He is looking forward to the arrival of the Emperor of Russia and the King of Prussia. Meanwhile the forts round Paris are being strengthened and the work is nearly finished. Yesterday morning a train reached the Saint-Denis railroad station filled with siege guns.

There was an explosion of pacific confidence at the Bourse with greatly rising prices. It is said that the financial houses have been buying on a considerable scale.

C. de B., 27th April 1867.

The emperor considers that peace is made, but Napoleon is trying to shift responsibility for his diplomatic defeats on Benedetti, his minister in Berlin, whom he accuses of making three grave errors:

1. That he failed to inform his Government of the true state of the Prussian military machine prior to the war against Austria in 1866.

2. That he did not inform the emperor quickly enough of the military treaties between Prussia and the States of southern Germany.

3. That he did not warn the emperor of the bad impression in Berlin that would be caused by his demands for Luxemburg.

C. de B., 2nd May 1867.

Bismarck, encouraged by the turn of events, took an even stronger line.

M. de Bismarck has sent a telegram to his ambassador, Goltz, in which he says: 'The armaments being built up by the French

Government are a menace which obliges me to say: "I will not tolerate them."'

When this matter was brought to the attention of the French Government, M. de Moustier telegraphed to our ambassador in Berlin: 'Assure M. de Bismarck that rumours of our armaments are the invention of malevolent people whose object is to provoke discord. Beg him not to believe a word.'

C. de B., 11th May 1867.

The simultaneous state visits of the Emperor of Russia and the King of Prussia in June made picturesque pageantry, marred by an attempt on the life of the Emperor Alexander which finally alienated Russia from the French cause. When Napoleon heard the pistol shot he whispered to the czar: 'If it's for me, it's an Italian.'

'And if it's for me,' answered the czar, 'it's a Pole.'

Napoleon and his ministers have noticed that the two sovereigns and their advisers were very careful to decide on all matters of mutual interest *before* coming to Paris. Thus the King of Prussia and Bismarck did not leave Berlin until they had arranged details of the customs treaty with the south German States and the Grand Duke of Baden had signed his treaty with Prussia on the eve of his departure for France. The Emperor of Russia and King William, before leaving for the court of the Tuileries, held long conferences in Berlin to fix the details of their political programme. The visiting princes, therefore, faced the French Government with a *fait accompli*, and never asked its advice on anything.

The theory of *faits accomplis*, like those of non-intervention and the principles of nationalities, are accordingly turned against that Government which first advanced them. It was in the name of non-intervention that the French Cabinet was forced to evacuate Syria, Rome, and Mexico, and to abandon the confederate States of the south. The *faits accomplis* triumphed in the duchies of the Elbe and in Germany to the detriment of France and her policy of nationalities! C. de B., 20th June 1867.

Just as the visiting sovereigns had discussed matters by themselves before arriving in Paris, so the King of Prussia decided to stop at Brussels on his way back to Berlin, and talk to the King of the Belgians, whose heir had married a Hohenzollern earlier in the year. These talks were so successful that Belgium promised to remain neutral in the event of a Franco-Prussian war.

Presently the Queen of Prussia came to Paris, to be received by the emperor at the Tuileries with every mark of affection.

The Queen of Prussia, in the course of her visit to Paris, is taking infinite pains to assure Napoleon of the friendly relations between Berlin and Paris. She has had several long talks with Napoleon III, and has gone out of her way to persuade him that Prussia is in a state of evolution, and admirably fitted to come to a close understanding with France. She says that Austria's policy is more and more directed away from Europe and towards the Near East.

Napoleon III has not wanted to show himself averse to an alliance with Prussia, but he has pointed out what he has already said to Bismarck, that the French Government is obliged to be careful of public opinion, and that it is therefore necessary to be particularly prudent. Even Prussia would be wise to act cautiously in its plans for the unification of Germany so as not to excite French suspicions unduly. C. de B., 15th July 1867.

Both in court circles and amongst highly placed officials here everybody is struck by the increased virulence of Prussian newspaper attacks against the imperial Government. Every day officials of the Ministry of Foreign Affairs seize a large number of foreign newspapers. A summary of foreign criticisms is compiled, however, for the emperor and his principal Cabinet ministers by the Ministry of the Interior. No doubt exists therefore about the hostile and disdainful tone of the German press towards our Government.

A striking incident took place at the agricultural exhibition at Billancourt, showing quite clearly Prussia's intentions.

The Prussian commissary at the International Tournament of Draught Horses was praising the superior merits of his country's horses. When the French commissary put forward the qualities of French horses, the Prussian officer lost his temper and ended by saying: 'It matters little whether or not you appreciate our German horses, for we shall be bringing them to drink in the river Seine in a few months' time! C. de B., 29th July 1867.

There remains no doubt in official circles that war will break out with Germany, though we are not yet ready. Only a quarter of the army is issued with the new Chassepot rifles, but there is a feeling that time is on our side. C. de B., 2nd August 1867.

Prussia is determined to make war rather than to halt in her movement of infiltrations. Napoleon admits when talking to his intimate friends that he is passing through a most difficult moment, both in home and in foreign politics, and that he cannot yet see how he is going to get out of the wood.

The Cabinet of the Tuileries is watching with mistrust the British expedition into Abyssinia. If the British stay there they will then dominate the Red Sea, Egypt, and the Suez Canal, which we appear to have made more for their benefit than for ours. C. de B., 21st September 1867.

Some surprise was caused in Paris by the fact that Napoleon, in spite of his dictatorial powers, allowed M. Rouher, his Minister of State, and Marshal Niel to make speeches containing diametrically opposed views on the great issue of peace and war. The truth is that the emperor at this moment showed less confidence in his own judgment.

In June 1868 the emperor and the empress paid a visit to Rouen.

Everybody who was at Rouen on Sunday noticed how sad, how tired, and how morose the emperor appeared.

When the empress was visiting the exhibition of flowers she turned to the prefect and exclaimed: 'How wilted they are!'

'Ah! madame,' answered the prefect, 'they were fresh this morning. It is the sun that has wilted them.'

The empress exclaimed: 'It is just like the gown one wears at a ball, fresh in the morning, wilted at the end of the evening.'

Never before have the intimate conversations of people in high positions shown such a lack of confidence. Everywhere there is despondency and uneasiness, in spite of an outward appearance of calm, over the situation at home and abroad.

People see the emperor placed in a position of being unable to go either forwards or backwards without meeting equal danger.   C. de B., June 1868.

In his speech from the throne in 1868 Napoleon had declared that France's military strength was equal to her needs. Bismarck knew otherwise. And so, for that matter, did Napoleon.

It is difficult to understand why the emperor, who used his dictatorial powers so readily on occasion, never imposed total rearmament when it was clearly a matter of life and death for the nation.

Yet there were moments after Sadowa when he was on the point of doing so.[1] In October 1866 he summoned a series of conferences, first at Saint-Cloud, later at Compiègne, at which his ministers, his marshals, and his chief generals were present. Napoleon claimed that it was indispensable to have, like Prussia, a million men under arms. Most of the politicians said that the Chamber would not agree, and Randon was quite satisfied with the army as it was. Niel put up a compromise scheme that was better than nothing.

Now why did not Napoleon thump his fist on the table and lay down his will? If the chamber proved difficult, was not the emperor able to dissolve it? Napoleon ended by supporting Niel's scheme, though he was unable to prevent it from being severely mauled in committee. Meanwhile Randon had been removed from the Ministry of War and Niel put in his place.

Niel's scheme was debated in public session in December 1867. Jules Favre, who was to have an inglorious meeting with the King of Prussia and Bismarck at Ferrières in 1870 asking for an armistice, cried out during this session:

'I am certain that the strongest nation will prove to be the one that is nearest to disarmament.'

Later he cried:

'Do you want to turn France into a monster barracks?'

[1] *Le Second Empire*, par Octave Aubry, pp 484–91. Paris, 1938.

21

Marshal Niel answered grimly:

'Take care you do not turn it into a cemetery!'

Émile Ollivier exclaimed:

'The armies of France have, to my mind, always been too large. Now they will cost us an exorbitant sum. Why? What is the necessity? Where is the peril? Who threatens us?'

.   .   .   .   .   .

Mme de Pourtalès, passing through Strasburg on her return from Germany, called on General Ducrot, who was to play a distinguished role in the war to come. She confided to him the things she had seen and learned. War was inevitable, and the Prussians were getting ready for it with such speed and with such intelligence that they were certain of victory.

'Come, come!' put in General Ducrot, feigning a dash of irony. 'You tell me this at the precise moment when on all sides people are talking of the pacific intentions of our good neighbours, of the terror we are supposed to impose upon them, and when we are demobilizing so many of our soldiers that I myself am preparing to go and cultivate my garden in the Nivernais!'

'These Prussians,' said Mme de Pourtalès, 'are cheating us infamously, and are planning to spring on us while we are unarmed. In public Germans speak of their peaceful intentions and of their desire to live in friendly relations with us; but when, in private, one speaks to those in close touch with the King of Prussia, they assume a sly, sarcastic tone, and say:

'"Do you believe all that? Can you not see that events are moving swiftly, and that nothing is any longer able to prevent what is about to happen?"

'These people deride us and despise our Government, our army, and our emperor, claiming that very soon France will be a second Spain.

Comtesse de Pourtalès. From a Painting by Winterhalter

'And would you believe that the Minister of the Royal House-hold dared to tell me to my face that our Alsace would belong to Prussia within eighteen months? And if you knew what immense preparations are everywhere being carried out; with what ardour the Prussians are working to transform and to wield together the armies of the states they have recently annexed; what confidence reigns in all ranks of society and the army. Truly, general, I have come back broken-hearted, distressed, and consumed with fear.'

Mme de Pourtalès later repeated her words to Napoleon III at Compiègne. The emperor listened until she had finished speaking, and then said:

'Countess, your lovely blue eyes have seen things through the prism of your imagination—things that do not exist. Believe me, we have nothing to fear from Prussia.'

II. THE INTRODUCTION CONTINUED

EARLY in the tragic year of 1870 Napoleon III entrusted Émile Ollivier with the formation of a Cabinet. Ollivier, passionately keen to give a new lease of life to the regime, decided to gather young men about him.

'We will give the emperor a happy old age,' he rather naïvely remarked to a friend who, having just left Napoleon III, spoke of his drawn features. The political machine prevented Ollivier from collecting youthful talent. White-haired, round-faced Comte Daru became Foreign Minister. 'I want peace,' he declared, and to prove it he informed Lord Clarendon that France was ready to cut down the size of her army. To test Prussian reaction Lord Loftus, British ambassador in Berlin, was instructed by the Foreign Office to call on Bismarck, but the chancellor answered: 'Our respective military systems are too different; control would be impossible.' The French military attaché in Berlin remarked: 'Prussia is not a country with an army, but an army that has a country.'

Six months later the Legislative Body was still vaguely discussing military man-power. Then, on 2nd July, the *Gazette de France* printed the news that Madrid's dictator, Marshal Prim, intended to offer the throne of Spain to a Hohenzollern.

That was the spark that lit the Franco-Prussian War. Throughout all the shifting and shuffling that led, by way of Bismarck's famous Ems telegram, to France's declaration of war on Germany, Napoleon must bear his share of responsibility.

There was war fever in the Chamber and on the boulevards. It was to be found in Napoleon's entourage, and on this occasion the Empress Eugénie's advice was deplorable. Yes, the public might have been disappointed if there had been no war, but not nearly so disappointed as Bismarck. It was the chancellor's crowning diplomatic success that he succeeded in placing the responsibility for the war—that was *his* war—on Napoleon.

Émile Ollivier read a message to the Senate on 15th July, and his words were a clear warning that war was to be declared. Enthusiasm was so high that Thiers had considerable difficulty in making himself heard when he rose to speak. Imperialists and Republicans tried to shout him down. The Marquis de Piré cried:

'You are an unpatriotic trumpet of disaster!'

Thiers flung back:

'Remember May 1866. You did not listen when I pointed out the danger then. That should suffice to make you listen to me now. . . . I regard this war as supremely unwise. I desire vengeance for Sadowa as much as any of you, but I consider the occasion extremely ill chosen.'

For the first few days hopes ran high. There was the picture, easily conjured up, of the Napoleonic eagle spreading its wings again over German territory. Nobody guessed the utter unpreparedness and lack of material in the French army. Even the Prussians appear to have been surprised. Napoleon III was suffering torture from his illness. Earlier in the month five specialists were called to Saint-Cloud, and they had even discussed the advisability of an operation, but the emperor, knowing that an operation of the same kind had caused the death of Marshal Niel, was not inclined to take the risk.

He braced himself up, exclaiming: 'Am I not a Napoleon?' entrained at Saint-Cloud for Metz, and waving farewell to the Empress Eugénie, his ministers, and his intimate friends, took a last long look at Paris, where he had known such glory, and which he now saw for the last time.

The skirmish at Saarbrücken, when the Prince Imperial received his baptism of fire, gave false hope to Parisians. Soon, alas, came Wissembourg, Forbach, Wörth . . . disastrous pages in this sublime epic.

The Chamber was summoned by decree. Thiers and Gambetta clamoured for a defence committee, which was persistently refused by General de Palikao, the new Prime Minister. In different ways Thiers and Gambetta were to play leading roles in the future of France—Thiers, the spectacled, white-haired septuagenarian, Gambetta, the youthful Republican, whose one idea was to pursue the war to a bitter end.

On 13th August Gambetta mounted the tribune, and took from his pocket a Nancy paper, which described how the city was captured by four Prussian soldiers. His rich voice was husky as he shouted:

'We are in the hands of incompetents!'

A few days later he read a cutting from the *Progrès de la Marne* announcing that Châlons was captured by only five Prussian cavalrymen.

On Sunday, 4th September, following a Cabinet meeting, presided over by General de Palikao, a proclamation was issued telling the French people of the disaster of Sedan. The news was conveyed in a telegram from the emperor, now a prisoner, to the empress the previous afternoon. Already on the Saturday evening the public knew that the Prussian forces were marching on Paris, and the Place de la Concorde was filled with people, to whom Gambetta appealed for patience so that the Assembly might deliberate in peace. The Chamber held an all-night sitting during which Jules Favre and Gambetta called for the overthrow of Louis-Napoleon and his dynasty and the nomination of a defence committee. The Chamber adjourned at midday on Sunday without reaching a decision.

When the Chamber met again in the early afternoon Palikao suggested a council of defence, with himself as lieutenant-general. He made no mention of the emperor. Thiers got up and offered an amendment which came half-way between the motions of Palikao and Jules Favre, but meanwhile another huge crowd formed in the Place de la Concorde, and this time it broke through the cordon and poured into the Palais-Bourbon. From thousands of throats came a demand for the deposition of the emperor and the setting up of a Republic.

Gambetta mounted the tribune and facing the crowd appealed for calm, but his voice was drowned in cries of 'Long live the Republic!'

Who pretended not to hear this popular clamour for a Republic?

None other than this impetuous Republican. So immense was the issue that he appeared frightened of grappling with it. But as he called for calm again and answered the crowd, he agreed that the Napoleonic dynasty was ended. The shouting doubled in volume, and as the public swarmed up the steps of the tribune and jostled into the seats reserved for the deputies, the query went up louder and louder:

'But what about the Republic?'

Jules Favre elbowed his way through and shouted:

'Do you or do you not want a civil war?'

'No, no. We want to fight the Prussians.'

Jules Favre raised his voice and made this non-committal answer:

'The Republic? It is not here that we must proclaim it.'

Then, seeing the possibilities of clearing the Chamber he quickly added:

'Yes. Long live the Republic. Citizens, let us proclaim it at the Hôtel de Ville!'

Gambetta and Jules Favre climbed down from the tribune, and shouting 'To the Hôtel de Ville!' led the way out of the Palais-Bourbon. Under a broiling sun Jules Favre and Jules Ferry marched at the head of one half of the surging crowd by way of the right bank of the Seine; Gambetta and Ernest Picard, at the head of the other half, by the left bank. It was half-past three.

Thiers and those deputies who had remained in the Chamber decided to take up the various motions where they had left them off, and discuss them in greater detail. The events of the last hour appeared to them as nothing more than a rowdy interlude.

They had just reached a negative formula when Jules Favre returned to tell them that a Provisional Government had been constituted at the Hôtel de Ville by the public. There were angry protests from the Right, but Thiers pointed out that it was wise to accept what had happened. He advised them to retire with dignity.

The Legislative Body thus came to an end.

The revolution would have been incomplete or might at least have led to bloodshed if the co-operation of the army had not been obtained. General Trochu, Governor of Paris, was asked to become president of the Provisional Government, and this good Catholic and excellent family man, having first consulted his wife, was wise enough to accept.

Jules Favre became Foreign Minister, Gambetta, Minister of the Interior, Ernest Picard, Finance Minister, and Le Flô, War Minister.

Trochu, wiry, with the features of a vulture, was a soldier and a Breton. Only fifty-five years old at the outbreak of war, he should have been given high command in the field, for he served with distinction in the Crimean War and in the Italian campaign, but his brochure, *The French Army in 1867* (first published anonymously), annoyed Napoleon, and he was retired on half-pay. The book was a warning that the French army was not sufficiently modern. It made a great stir, and Bismarck studied it with care. It ended with the words:

'We have gone to sleep in self-satisfaction; we have turned away from hard work, neglecting real effort, research, and comparison with other armies, though all these things are necessary to progress. We must prepare ourselves resolutely for the task that lies ahead.'

On 17th August 1870 the emperor had appointed Trochu

Governor of Paris and Commander-in-Chief of the armed forces
destined to defend the capital, but this choice was not altogether
voluntary. It was imposed on Napoleon by the military.

The revolutionaries of September in making Trochu their
president chose an Orleanist. This suggests that they did not
believe that France was yet ready for a full-blooded republic.

The siege of Paris began on 19th September.

On the same day King William, Bismarck, and Moltke arrived
at the château of Ferrières, the country estate of the Rothschilds.

King William took possession of the private apartments of
the Baron Alphonse; Bismarck those of the Baron James, while
Moltke occupied those of the Baroness James. The King of
Prussia brought his own cooks, and the estate supplied everything that was necessary—game, fruit, and flowers. The royal
suite included 3,000 men and 1,200 horses, quartered both at
Ferrières itself and in the village.

Within a few days Jules Favre, in his capacity of Foreign
Minister in the Government of National Defence, arrived at the
château. He was hoping to obtain terms that did not involve
any loss of territory. The Republicans, so suddenly thrust into
office, found it difficult to realize the extent of the nation's
disaster. Jules Favre was genuinely surprised at the cold and
contemptuous attitude of the King of Prussia. Bismarck, in
return for an armistice, demanded the immediate occupation of
Strasburg and one of the main forts of Paris. Favre returned
to Paris, where the Government of National Defence valiantly
decided to go on with the war. The French staff at Ferrières
watched the departure of Jules Favre with heavy hearts. They
had intended to plant a young tree to commemorate the peace!

Trochu proved himself a master of passive resistance during
the siege. MacMahon's army was imprisoned in Germany,
that of Bazaine was besieged in Metz; General Vinoy was trying to bring back to Paris some 16,000 men. Trochu had a

considerable army under his command. It was made up of regulars, Mobiles, and National Guards.

Gambetta was of the opinion that the Government should not stay in the besieged capital. A compromise was reached whereby the head of the Government would remain while a few members were sent to Tours. The provinces were starting movements of their own.

The Prussians cut the cable between Paris and Tours on 25th September, and a few days later Gambetta was asked to go to Tours. At first he refused, saying that as he was the youngest member of the Government he wished to remain where the danger was greatest. His colleagues, who were anxious for him to go on political grounds, pointed out that the journey by air might prove just as dangerous as staying in Paris. Gambetta answered:

'I will come back with an army, and if I have the glory of delivering Paris, I will ask nothing more of destiny.'

He left Montmartre in a balloon at eleven o'clock on 7th October. This balloon, the *Armand Barbès*, was shot at by the Prussians just after it had cleared the fortifications of Paris. It was then at a height of only six hundred metres, and the bullets whistled by.

A quarter of an hour later it landed in a turnip field, but rose again by a miracle, and was driven by a light wind in a northerly direction towards Creil, where the Germans shot at it a second time. Gambetta was wounded in the hand, but not seriously, and the balloon landed safely near Montdidier in the Somme after covering ninety-eight kilometres in four and a half hours.

The *Armand Barbès* could hardly have taken a route more opposed to Gambetta's destination. Tours is south-west of Paris; Montdidier is north-east. Gambetta took advantage of his presence in the north to go as far as Rouen to see what conditions were like in Normandy, and to receive a deputation of patriots, who presented him with an address. 'Self-sacrifice abounds, but energetic leadership is missing. Be in the provinces what you have been in Paris . . . and France will be saved.'

Gambetta's journey brings us to an interesting aspect of the C. de B. letters—the way in which they were sent out of the capital.

The balloon post was born of necessity. Paris found itself suddenly cut off from the outside world. A few couriers were successful in crossing the Prussian lines, but so few that as time went on it became practically impossible to find men willing to take the risk. They feared to be shot as spies. C. de B. tells of one who was seized and who narrowly escaped death. A letter found amongst the C. de B. correspondence written by a man in Paris to his agent at Le Havre tells of failure to find a single courier in the capital.

'You will doubtless find a courier more easily at Le Havre. You should pay him 500 francs or even 1,000 francs for the journey, but only a small amount of this sum should be paid at the time of his departure.'

One thousand francs, then £40, was a considerable sum. Many men did not earn as much in a year.

The function of the balloon was to carry passengers and mail over the Prussian lines into unoccupied territory, but once the aeronaut had taken off he had no idea where he would eventually land. The first departure took place from the Place Saint-Pierre in Montmartre on 23rd September, which was the fifth day of the siege. The balloon, called the *Neptune*, landed at Craconville, near Évreux (Eure), having covered 104 kilometres in three and a half hours. It carried 250 pounds of mail. The journey was so successful that two decrees, dated 26th September, were issued, giving instructions for the new postal service. The maximum weight for a letter was four grammes, and the charge was twenty centimes for France and Algeria, and the usual letter rate for foreign countries. Letters had to be written on a special paper, so thin as to be almost transparent. Generally the sheet was folded in such a way that the address could be written on the outer fold. C. de B. was an exception in that he used an envelope.

Balloons, nearly all of which bore names, left every few days, occasionally twice a day. One or two travelled great distances, like the *Ville d'Orléans*, that on 24th November came down in Norway. The *Ville de Paris* (15th December) landed in Prussia! A few came to rest in Holland and others in Belgium, but apart from one that fell in the sea near Plymouth, and another lost in the Bay of Arcachon, accidents were rare.

The letters sent out this way bear the inscription 'Ballon Monté.' This means that there was an aeronaut in charge and that there were passengers as well as mail. A scheme for sending up paper balloons with a load of post cards was not a success. The first one, released on 30th September, fell in the German lines a mile and a half outside Paris.

The 'Ballon Monté' became so popular that enterprising firms made little news-sheets of flimsy paper. The first two pages contained the latest news printed in small type. The third page was left blank for a personal letter by the sender, and the fourth was set aside for the address when the sheet was folded. The total weight did not exceed the four grammes.

The chief news-sheet was called the *Gazette des Absents*. It appeared three times a week, and the printed matter contained the military communiqués, latest decrees, short extracts from the newspapers, and the last-minute prices on the Bourse.

Each balloon carried a number of pigeons, for the problem of bringing news into Paris was infinitely more complicated than that of sending it out. The *Armand Barbès*, in which Gambetta left, took sixteen pigeons to bring back the young revolutionary's messages. When none arrived there was great anxiety at Trochu's headquarters. The average number of pigeons carried was six, though the *Général Ulrich* (18th November) landed at Pontoise with thirty-four.

As time went on a system was devised whereby each pigeon could carry a great quantity of very thin sheets of collodion.

The messages were reduced to infinitesimal size by photography —the forerunners of the 'airgraph' service inaugurated by General Wavell for troops in the Near East in 1941.

As soon as the first passenger and mail balloons to leave Paris were sighted by the Prussians, Moltke sent a messenger to Krupp urging him to invent an anti-balloon gun. Though rifle bullets occasionally whistled past a balloon flying low—as in the case of the *Armand Barbès*—Moltke realized that a much more powerful weapon must be invented. Krupp produced the 'balloon musket,' which was the first anti-aircraft gun. Tissandier has described in detail how the gun was made to swing vertically and horizontally, how there was a seat for the gunner just behind it, and how the whole thing was mounted on a light platform on four wheels drawn, when necessary, by two horses to the scene of action. Several French aeronauts claimed to have heard shots from this gun at heights of between 800 and 1,000 metres. The only proven hits were registered on the *Daguerre*, which, on 12th November 1870, was obliged to make a forced landing at Ferrières, where the passengers were made prisoners by Prussian cavalry.

Nearly all the Diplomatic Corps left Paris before the siege, though the United States and Swiss ministers remained until the end, together with the military attachés of the Russian Embassy, who made journeys between Paris and Tours to report to their Government. Foreign diplomats passed by permission through the Prussian lines, though these journeys were not always without risk.

Thiers, who had left Paris before the siege to visit London, Vienna, and St Petersburg in a vain attempt to obtain foreign aid, returned with a Prussian safe-conduct towards the end of October in order to negotiate the preliminaries of an armistice with Bismarck.

The Siege of Paris had certain aspects that are remarkably topical. The Spitfire Fund after the Battle of Britain in 1940 was not so very different from the Giant Cannon Fund of October 1870, when thousands of private people, organizations, and Government departments subscribed for their own cannon to defend Paris. The postal employees called theirs the 'Telegraph,' and on it were engraved the words:

'Neither an inch of our territory nor a stone of our fortresses.'

A black-out of the city was decreed as soon as it became clear that the enemy intended to carry out systematic bombardments. For days and nights shells fell on thickly populated quarters of Paris. Buildings were flattened out, and a number of people killed and injured. The Prussians did not make these bombardments for any military reason. It was merely an attempt to demoralize the civilian population.

The only result has been to kill harmless civilians, old people, women, and children; to destroy buildings and houses, and to kindle amongst Parisians sentiments of vengeance. Last night, from 10 p.m. to 4 a.m., the frightened population never went to bed. Women ran out of the houses that were hit, clutching their children in their arms. It was a spectacle of desolation, but also of anger, especially on the part of the women.

C. de B.

When Trochu visited the damage the population called for reprisals. The general, whose policy had hitherto been mainly one of passive resistance, was obliged to resume the offensive. The continued bombardment sent Parisians down to their cellars. They slept there at night, played cards below ground, and only ventured out between the salvos to pick up pieces of jagged hot metal for souvenirs.

The food shortage was perhaps the most serious aspect of the siege. In an unpublished letter written by a Parisian to his evacuated wife in the department of the Indre on 9th January there is this description:

'If, my dear Augusta, I have had many reasons since 13th August to regret my decision to send you and my small children away into the country, I am now satisfied that I was wise to do so. It is beginning to rain old iron on Paris.

'I must say that one finds it almost easier to become accustomed to shells (which, like railway locomotives, whistle before arriving

34

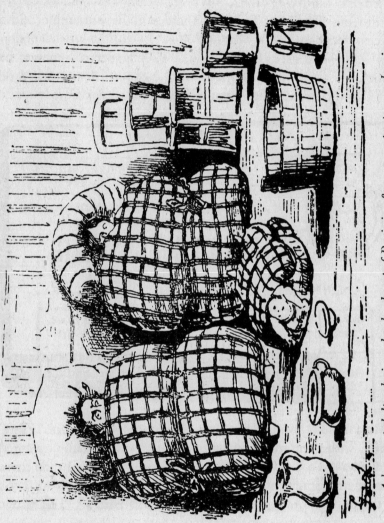

A basement shelter during a bombardment of Paris in 1870—a contemporary drawing

at their destination) than to eating horse-flesh. I cannot get any more used to eating horse than dog or rat. I dined last night on camel. We are eating the inmates of the Jardin des Plantes. To-night there will be porcupine and a piece of elephant trunk (that of Polluse, one of the little elephants that our kids used to ride on). Elephant costs twenty-six francs a pound. Let's hope it will be good. It is a rare food but I would prefer fried potatoes and a piece of cheese.'

Although rationing was only introduced slowly and reluctantly, with great inequalities, food cards were actually invented by General Trochu. At first more cards were issued than there were members of families, but when this was discovered a census of the population was taken and new cards issued. The public utility concerns were also rationed. Gas, which meant not only heating but lighting, was curtailed, and then cut off.

Jules Favre sent the Comte de Chaudordy to Tours as Director of Foreign Affairs. Chaudordy was a live wire, intelligent and supple, who had previously been principal private secretary to Drouyn de Lhuys. He protested, on 29th November, against German atrocities, placing on record many acts of cruelty. Hospitals were broken into, and the wounded burned in their beds. Frenchmen were carried off to Germany to work for the aggressor.

The armistice that Jules Favre was unable to arrange at Ferrières in September was negotiated at Versailles on 28th January 1871.

The elections of the National Assembly took place on 8th February. We shall find these described in detail by C. de B. The armistice convention stipulated that the Assembly should decide whether the war was to go on or under what conditions peace should be signed.

This was the issue on which France voted. Paris and many of the provincial cities voted with Gambetta, the champion of war to the bitter end. The rural districts voted for peace. It was the peace party that won; but upon whom did the country call to give it peace? To the Legitimists and the Orleanists.

Thus, five months after the crowds in the Place de la Concorde had shouted for a Republic, the nation sent to the Chamber a huge Royalist majority. What had happened to the Republicans?

The truth is that the great majority of Frenchmen were suspicious of Republicanism. The word left a nasty taste in the mouth. It recalled the blood baths of 1789 and 1848, the guillotine and the street barricades. No glory had come to exalt its name. There was none of the halo that later crowned it by reason of its colonial conquests and the victorious war of 1914–1918. Just now it was the war party, and a war party without a chance of being successful because the enemy was installed everywhere. Gambetta's passionate ardour, his heated speeches, frightened reasonable people, who longed for an antidote to famine and carnage.

The elections threw into power a national hero. This was Thiers—the man of 1866, the wise, white-haired veteran, who had replaced his aggressiveness of the time of Sadowa with a cautious cunning. His policy was not to hit his head against a steel wall of Prussian bayonets, but to negotiate so skilfully that he would end by getting the better of his adversary. Whatever secret sympathy Thiers had for young Gambetta, he called him in public 'that furious madman.'

Until 4th September Thiers was nominally an Orleanist. Politically he was akin to Trochu. Now he was moving towards a cautious Republicanism. As soon as the National Assembly met at Bordeaux it appointed Thiers to be Chief of Executive Power, that is to say, head of the State. So Royalist was this Chamber that Thiers had to insist that his title of Chief of Executive Power should be followed by the words 'of the French Republic.'

The peace treaty was a blow to Gambetta. Disgusted, he went to Spain for a rest. The extreme Left did not cease to bewail the loss of Alsace and Lorraine, torn from the motherland. The leaders of this outcry were Louis Blanc, Edgar Quinet, Victor Hugo, and Georges Clemenceau, who was to nurse his revenge until 1918, never forgetting, never forgiving.

We often find C. de B. rather bitter against these men. He seldom alludes to Gambetta, for instance, except with the prefix of 'citoyen,' which has a tinge of sarcasm; but, as with Thiers, C. de B.'s main concern was to get rid of the Germans. The Republic might never have lived had it been left to the extremists.

The Prussians made a two days' occupation of Paris. These forty-eight hours are poignantly described in the letters. 1st March and 2nd March and the morning of 3rd March 1871 were a bitter prelude to the desecration of 1940. The German technique was only in the infancy of its refined cruelty. Parisians remained behind closed doors in a dignified aloofness. They retained their self-respect.

For rather more than a fortnight after the Germans evacuated

Paris the heart of the city throbbed uncertainly. The National Assembly was to meet at Versailles on 20th March. The Commune broke out on 18th March.

What was this appalling revolt? Fundamentally it was an expression of suppressed anger on the part of the public against the peace terms. The public longed to do something, to rise furiously against the insolent Hun. They were paying for the passive years before the war.

The movement that was born of patriotism developed into infamy. Those who wanted to strike at the enemy helped him by creating civil war at home. Bismarck watched cynically, and told Thiers that if the French Government could not quell the Commune German troops would be called to restore order. The Prussian war lord was offering protective custody.

When the situation became serious in Paris, C. de B. went to Versailles, or rather escaped there in a stream of refugees. The move was necessary because he could no longer send his daily dispatches from the capital.

Thiers now organized the loyal troops in their fight against the Communards. When he had broken the Commune, and his army of Versailles entered Paris, who meted out savage retribution? The septuagenarian who was always being accused of timidity.

III. THE END OF THE INTRODUCTION

THE Communards made their last stand in the cemetery of Père la Chaise on 28th May. It was the final blood bath, out of which the young Republic emerged cleansed of its inflammatory character. Henceforth the Republic was Thiers. That is to say, it put on the cloak of respectability. It was moderate, clean, and proper. The middle classes did not shun it.

Although the last Germans had not yet left the soil, it was clear that more peaceful days were in sight. The convulsions that necessarily follow a crushing defeat were dying down. Thiers, more than anybody, knew that this was no time to relax, and he was determined to keep his grip on national affairs as strong as it had ever been. He became less and less willing to delegate power, and this made him so autocratic that C. de B. quotes the gibe of the Monarchist Buffet, one of the Conservative leaders in the National Assembly, which was then sitting at Versailles:

I am surrounded by portraits of Louis XIV, and if this monarch still lived I should probably find it easier to speak to him than to M. Thiers!

And again:

He who during his long career has not ceased to attack all forms of personal government, has become the most personal government ever known. His ministers complain that not one of them is able to take any decision without having consulted M. Thiers, and that he always claims to know more about a question than the minister concerned. In this he is probably often right. C. de B., 18th July 1871.

The fact that Thiers and the Republic were synonymous was in itself a danger to the regime. It was by no means certain at this

40

stage that, if Thiers were overthrown, the young Republic could survive.

What then would emerge?

The Bonapartists were not a real menace any longer. There might be a few rural districts where Napoleon III was regretted, but in the cities only a handful of former senators, judges, and civil servants, who had lost their livelihood since the overthrow of the Second Empire, would have welcomed his return.

Even Napoleon himself was not yet ready to make any plans. When one of his partisans visited him in England, in October 1871, he found Napoleon depressed and in bad health. Asked what plans he had for a restoration, Napoleon answered that he would only return if he were called by a plebiscite. Reminded of Strasburg and Boulogne, Napoleon said:

One does such things in youth. I am neither able nor willing to attempt a *coup d'état*.
C. de B.

No; what was really at the back of most people's minds was the possibility of a monarchy.

The Royalist majority in the National Assembly included the Legitimists, who rallied behind the Comte de Chambord, descendant of Louis XIV, and the Orleanists, who rallied behind the Comte de Paris, descendant of Monsieur, only brother of Louis XIV.

The only way to understand this question is to go back to an August evening in 1715, when the great King Louis XIV lay dying. Here is the historic description handed down by the monarch's valet, Anthoine:

'Louis XIV, having received the extreme unction, sent for Philippe d'Orléans, his only brother's son, and had a conversation with him that lasted for a quarter of an hour. His Majesty enjoined him in all things to have religion, adding: "I commend to you the Dauphin. Serve him as faithfully as you have served me; do your best to preserve the kingdom for him; if he were to disappear you would be the master. I know your goodness of

41

heart, your wisdom, your courage, and the wide range of your character. I am satisfied that you will watch carefully over the good education of the Dauphin, and that you will omit nothing for the solace of the people of his kingdom. . . . My dear nephew, keep your memory of me green. I have made those arrangements that I believe to be the wisest and the most equitable for the good of the kingdom; but as no man is able to foresee everything, if there is something to change or to reform, that which is necessary must be done."

'The prince, having answered the king, knelt with tears in his eyes, kissed the sovereign twice, and received his benediction.

'Louis XIV died on 1st September.

'All those who were great in the kingdom entered the apartments of Philippe d'Orléans to salute him as the regent. . . . He led the courtiers to the feet of the new king, Louis XV, aged five years, and bowing low, said: "Sire, I come to render homage to you as the first of your subjects."

'The child was crying, but, seeing so much grace, smiled.

'His great-uncle had won his eternal friendship.'

Louis XV was succeeded in 1774 by his grandson, Louis XVI, whose little son, known as Louis XVII, was the martyr in the Temple during the Revolution.

Both brothers of Louis XVI were to reign after Napoleon's retreat from Moscow—Louis XVIII from 1814 to 1824 (except for the Hundred Days which began with Napoleon's return from Elba and which ended with his defeat at Waterloo); and Charles X from 1824 to 1830.

The Comte de Chambord was the only male descendant of this line.

In 1871 the Comte de Chambord was in his early fifties—a fat man, as corpulent as Louis XVIII; but whereas his great-uncle suffered from gout and was hardly able to walk, the Comte de Chambord was brisk and active. Fat from his youth, lame from a bad accident which happened when he was twenty-one, he made light of these infirmities.

It was during a holiday in Austria that Henri V, as the Legitimists called him, had his accident. He was staying with the Duc de Blacas, the business executive of all the Bourbons in exile. His horse shied at an ox-cart in a narrow defile, and the Comte de Chambord was thrown. He was tended by the same doctor who had watched both the Duc de Berry, his father, and Charles X, his grandfather, die.

The doctor sent for a specialist from Vienna who attached an iron ball to the injured leg to prevent it from being shorter than the other. The remedy proved worse than the ill.

At the outbreak of the war of 1870 the Comte de Chambord left Frohsdorf, the château in Austria where he spent much of his exile, for the nearest point in Switzerland to the French frontier. His idea was to raise an army of volunteers and attack the Germans on their flank, but the scheme proved impracticable.

Apart from a manifesto to the people of France in October 1870, Henri V remained inactive until the elections for the National Assembly in 1871.

When it was clear that the National Assembly had a large Royalist majority, a number of deputies went to see Thiers and asked pointedly:

'What about a restoration?'

The statesman answered:

'A monarchy if you will, but it must be a united monarchy.'

He knew that whereas the Legitimists and the Orleanists had voted as one during the elections, the Legitimists were quite a separate bloc in the National Assembly, and there was no reconciliation between the Bourbon and Orleanist pretenders. Thiers's views were now staunchly Republican. His policy was to prevent any accord between the two royal houses.

Conversely, the most urgent task for the Monarchists was to hasten the recognition by the Comte de Paris of Henri V.

The Comte de Paris was thirty-three years old, and a direct descendant of the regent, who received the death-bed recommendations of Louis XIV.

His grandfather was Louis-Philippe, the only member of the house of Orleans to mount the throne. Let us examine how he got there.

When, in 1830, Charles X, the last Bourbon king, was made to abdicate, he announced that the Dauphin, his only living son, simultaneously renounced his rights. Louis-Philippe was brought back to Paris to become lieutenant-general of the kingdom. Frenchmen now asked him to become their king.

But he hesitated.

The abdication of Charles X and of the Dauphin did not entirely eliminate the Bourbon line. There remained the posthumous ten-year-old son of the Duc de Berry, second son of Charles X.

This little boy was the Comte de Chambord.

Louis-Philippe, remembering the role of his ancestor, the regent, offered to remain lieutenant-general if the young Chambord (he was then known as the Duc de Bordeaux) were brought back to Paris and placed in his care.

This is how he planned the matter.[1]

An Englishman called Major Caradoc, later Lord Howden, was asked by the British ambassador, Lord Stuart, to see Louis-Philippe at the Palais-Royal. Louis-Philippe gave the Englishman a note, to be sewn in the lining of his coat, on which was written:

'To Charles X. Sire, believe what Major Caradoc tells you.'

Major Caradoc hurried to Normandy where, not far from Caen, he caught up with the dethroned Charles X and the royal cavalcade on its way to exile. The old monarch was affable; but the Duchesse de Berry, the Duc de Chambord's mother, refused to give up her son. When Major Caradoc came back to tell the news to the lieutenant-general, the head of the house of Orleans exclaimed:

[1] *Louis-Philippe*, par Denys Cochin (de l'Académie Française). Paris, 1918.

44

'Well, there's nothing left but for me to become king myself!'
He proved as home-loving a monarch as his ancestor, the
regent, was dissipated. Some people accused him of being mean,
but he pointed out the expense of bringing up a family of eight.

His five sons were Ferdinand-Philippe, who took the title of
Duc d'Orléans, the Duc de Nemours, the Prince de Joinville,
the Duc d'Aumale, and the Duc de Montpensier.

The Duc d'Orléans died in 1842. The Comte de Paris, his
eldest son, therefore became Orleanist pretender after the death
of Louis-Philippe in 1850.

There was only a Royalist majority in the National Assembly
if the Legitimists and Orleanists were counted together.

The Comte de Paris must therefore put himself entirely at the
disposal of Henri V, who was head of the senior branch—that
of the Bourbons.

Divided, they must of necessity fall. Together, the Orleanists
would automatically get back all their privileges.

The question arose whether the princes would be allowed
to come back to French soil whence they had been banished.
Thiers reluctantly consented.

The Prince de Joinville and the Duc de Chartres, the Comte
de Paris's younger brother, had both fought in the war of 1870.
The first, in order to circumvent the laws of exile, assumed an
American pseudonym, 'Colonel Lutteroth.' The second called
himself Robert le Fort. They were elected to the National
Assembly, but in return for Thiers's agreement to the abrogation
law promised not to sit. They were released from this promise
in 1872.

On Sunday, 2nd July 1871, the Brussels–Paris express steamed
into the almost deserted Gare du Nord at five o'clock in the
morning.[1]

Henri V, accompanied by the Comte de Monti, jumped out

[1] *Henri V*, par Pierre de Luz. Paris, 1931.

of the train. He was setting foot in Paris for the first time in forty-one years.

Carrying their bags, Henri V and his companion hired a closed cab, and asked to be driven to the church of Notre-Dame-des-Victoires, where they told the driver to wait. Unrecognized, they mingled with the congregation gathered for the celebration of mass.

Then they drove to Notre-Dame, where Henri V was baptized, and thence to the Tuileries, or rather what was left of it. Tears rolled down the cheeks of Henri V as he gazed on the charred ruins of the historic palace where he was born. The Commune had left its mark.

The cabby, watching his fare from the driving seat, shouted out good-humouredly:

'Cheer up, *bourgeois*, we'll build it up again!'

After Henri V had gazed for some time on the ruins of the Tuileries he asked to be driven to the home of his friend, the Baron de Nanteuil, in the Avenue de Villars, where he was to spend the day before going to his castle at Chambord.

The Marquis de la Ferté, Henri's representative at Versailles, told him he had seen the Comte de Paris, who expressed a desire to be received by his cousin.

The Comte de Paris was ready to recognize the principle of hereditary monarchy in the person of Henri V. This made him the Dauphin, because Henri had no children.

M. de la Ferté then raised the question of the white flag.

Henri V had repeatedly stated that his return to the throne was conditional upon the nation accepting the white flag of the kings of France. But many people, though prepared to support a monarchy, were not willing to give up the tricolour. Even the Orleanists did not consider the white flag at all necessary.

Now that the Comte de Paris was willing to recognize Henri V as the rightful king, M. de la Ferté realized that the question of the flag was the only remaining obstacle. He entreated Henri V not to insist, and a violent scene took place.

Napoleon III

Before leaving Paris that evening Henri V dictated a letter for his cousin.   He thanked him, but said that he was about to issue a manifesto, and that he thought it fairer to postpone the meeting until after that.

By November 1872 Thiers was thinking about a change in the parliamentary system.   The National Assembly was a single Chamber with sovereign powers.   So far it had proved docile to all his requests.   It had allowed him to reorganize the country and liberate the soil from German occupation.

Recovery had been rapid, and, because of this, those people who had turned to him for guidance when things looked bad now started to criticize because they were no longer afraid. Thiers said to himself: 'The National Assembly was a useful makeshift, but it cannot last.   I must leave something more permanent than this.'

To the members of the National Assembly he said:

'Your mission has been to save the country by procuring peace; after peace, order; then the re-establishment of the nation's strength and grandeur, and finally a regular Government.   Think over this matter, and if you require my advice I will give it to you loyally.'

Gambetta, in his *République Française*, hailed this statement with enthusiasm as preparing the way for a republic; but the Monarchists, who counted on the instability of the National Assembly for an eventual restoration, rose in arms.   Thiers was assailed.   He was accused of being a doddering old man. Things were said about his state of health and his dictatorial methods.   The National Assembly turned against him.   After attempting to tide over the storm by appointing a Committee of Thirty, Thiers was overthrown, and replaced by Marshal MacMahon.   The date was 24th May 1873.

Thiers's sacrifice was not in vain.

Because of the wide powers the country gave him in its hour of need, Thiers had governed from the tribune.   He was more or less a dictator. Marshal MacMahon, from without the Chamber, would apply the maxim:

'The president presides but does not govern.'

It was now that the Monarchists most nearly succeeded in placing Henri V on the throne.

On 3rd August 1873 Henri was taking his solitary afternoon stroll in the park at Frohsdorf when Vanssay, his gentleman-in-waiting, arrived with a telegram. It was from the Comte de Paris, and read:

'The Comte de Paris, having arrived last evening at Vienna, requests the gentleman-in-waiting to ask M. le Comte de Chambord when and where he will be kind enough to receive him.'

Henri read and re-read the telegram. It meant that the Comte de Paris was now not only prepared to offer his submission, but was willing to accept the principle of the flag which Henri raised in his manifesto from Chambord on 5th July 1871.

Vanssay hurried to Vienna, where the Comte de Paris received him personally.

'I desire,' he said, 'as quickly as possible to pay my respects to the head of the royal family.'

On 5th August Vanssay took the Comte de Paris to the château, where Henri V was waiting to receive him. The two princes remained closeted together for an hour, and the Comte de Paris stayed for lunch.

Reconciliation had taken place.

The question of the flag still barred the road, for although the principle was now accepted by the Comte de Paris, it was very doubtful whether the National Assembly would agree to it. In October a parliamentary committee was formed, and one of its members, Charles Chesnelong, was sent to Salzburg to confer with Henri V. A long and cordial discussion took place. Then Chesnelong exclaimed nervously:

'Ah, if we could only settle this question of the flag!'

'Never will I accept the tricolour,' answered Henri V.

Chesnelong, unwilling to face up to realities, said:

'Monseigneur will allow me not to have heard these words.'

For a fortnight after Chesnelong's return to Paris, where he gave the parliamentary committee an account of his visit, the members of the Right were so keen to restore the monarchy that they did not allow any unpleasant thoughts about the flag to interfere with their plans.

Henri's integrity, however, forbade him to allow any misunderstanding. He decided to force the issue. He wrote a letter to Chesnelong that was published in the press.

'It is the fashion to oppose the firmness of Henri V with the suppleness of Henri IV, who said: "The great love I bear to my subjects allows me to consider everything possible and even honourable." I agree; but I would like to know what lesson he would have meted out to the imprudent man who had tried to persuade him to renounce the standard of Arques and Ivry.'

The letter came as a bombshell.

The night it was made known Thiers was giving a reception at his home in the Faubourg Saint-Honoré.

'Standing beside his chimney,' wrote Alphonse Daudet's brother, Ernest, 'M. Thiers was radiant. He could not resist reading the letter aloud, and when he came to the passage about Arques and Ivry he stopped, looked at his guests from over his spectacles, and cried:

'"I'd like to see Pasquier's face!"'

The Duc d'Audiffret-Pasquier was the leading figure in the parliamentary committee that sent Chesnelong to see Henri V.

C. de B. says that the letter came to the Monarchist cause like 'a blow from an oar on a drowning man who thought he was within reach of the rescue boat.'

Many people wondered why Henri V refused a throne because of the colour of a flag.

49

But Henri's flag was a symbol of all that he stood for.

'If I had given way to the concessions demanded of me from the National Assembly,' said Henri V, 'I would probably have gained my throne for six months; but after that I would have been packed off once more into exile, and my second state would have been worse than my first.'

What exactly did he stand for?

The absolute monarchy of Louis XIV.

What did the National Assembly offer?

The establishment of a regime in which the king reigned, but did not govern; where all the major decisions lay with Parliament.

He was not a man to compromise. He could not bring himself to accept a ready-made constitution. The principle of heredity must be superior to the power of the National Assembly. That was his argument.

'Otherwise,' he said, 'there is no reason for my existence. If I am to be the legitimate king of the Revolution then I am no use at all, and without my principle I am only a fat man with a limp.'

In November Henri V returned to Paris. He sent M. de Blacas to Versailles to ask Marshal MacMahon, President of the Republic, to come and see him. The marshal refused, and so ended the last serious attempt to restore a monarchy.

The Conservatives once boasted that they would re-establish the throne even by one vote.

The Republic was confirmed by exactly that majority in January 1875, and lasted, in its new form, until the fateful summer of 1940.

From across the Rhine, Bismarck watched these events in anger. The German dream was for a divided France. Bismarck's propaganda had been busy during the last few years sowing distrust against both a republic and a monarchy. He feared a strong republic because it meant the reawakening of the nation. A monarchy was dangerous because it would lead to powerful alliances on the Continent.

Here was a Republic which, though born with difficulty, was now becoming prosperous. The shares rose on the Bourse, the wheels of industry turned at full speed, railroads and canals were built, money was plentiful. That spring Bismarck saw these things, and decided it was essential to break France's back once and for all. He planned to unleash his army against the country from which he had only just withdrawn.

But this time Europe was not willing to stand by and see another German aggression.

IV. THE OUTBREAK OF WAR

20TH *July 1870.* The French army yesterday began hostilities. As soon as the Prussian Government was notified of this it recalled its ambassador from Paris. The first secretary and the entire staff will leave at five o'clock this evening. M. Bamberg, the consul, will remain to settle the many commercial interests which affect the two countries.

The Imperial Guard started to move out of Paris yesterday. This, together with the decree appointing Marshal Lebœuf as Chief of Staff, indicates the emperor's imminent departure.

M. Émile Ollivier, who never doubts anything, has told the emperor he will be in Berlin within five days.

These are the military leaders in whom the emperor and the army have the greatest faith: Marshals MacMahon and Bazaine; Generals Bourbaki and Ladmirault.

Vessels that were due to leave Le Havre have received orders to remain in the harbour in case the Government needs them as troop carriers. The *Pereire* of the Compagnie Transatlantique, which was to leave for New York, has cancelled its sailing.

The Ministry of War has just received these details by telegraph from the Franco-German frontier:

The Prussians are massing near Trèves, but there is nothing yet to show that they are preparing to take the offensive. The Bavarian troops are holding noisy parades on their frontier.

A Cabinet meeting and a Council of War were held in Paris yesterday. The emperor appeared resolute and confident, and said:

'I shall sign the peace treaty at Königsberg. It is in that city that the kings of Prussia are crowned.'

10th August 1870. There is every reason to believe that the

German army has by now taken the offensive. The last five days have doubtless been used by the Prussian military leaders to unite the army corps of the king, of Prince Frederick Charles, and of the Crown Prince for an attack against Metz, which might simultaneously cut off our retreat on Nancy.

If we lose this battle the situation will be very serious, for we have no other army ready. Wounded officers back from the front claim that our army leaders are anxious for the emperor to abandon supreme command, but from official dispatches this morning it would seem that Napoleon has merely given Marshal Bazaine command of the army of Metz, and has retained command of the other army corps.

General Morin told his colleagues at the French Institute the other day that the emperor, during the first Council of War held at Metz to draw up a plan of campaign, presented one of his own. Though this plan was voted against by every expert present, the emperor insisted that it should be carried out.

A letter just arrived from G.H.Q. states that Napoleon III passed through a moment of despondency, but quickly recovered his self-confidence, becoming as cool and possessed as in the days when he was triumphant at the Palace of the Tuileries. The Ministry of War admits that 26,000 of our men were killed, 8,000 wounded, and 50,000 captured by the enemy at Forbach and at Wörth.

Princess Clotilde [daughter of King Victor Emmanuel] has received instructions from her husband, Prince Napoleon [brother of Princess Mathilde], to leave Meudon immediately and to take up residence at the Palais-Royal, with her trunks all packed, in case she is obliged to leave hurriedly.

The newspaper *Le Gaulois* publishes to-day a list of the men it supposes General de Palikao will call upon to form his Cabinet. The choice of this general is most unpopular. He must obviously play the role of a dictator, but one who will not last long if we suffer any more reverses.

The Besançon papers say that passenger and goods trains

between that city and Belfort have been cancelled since 8th August.

16th August 1870. More and more we are moving towards events that will decide the emperor's future. Our army, the only one that is organized at the present time, is falling back to fight a last battle under the walls of Paris. This army, together with the legion of ex-service men, will number some 200,000 against 400,000 to 500,000 Germans. If one could be sure that the French troops were properly led, they would certainly beat the Germans, but if this battle is lost we shall suffer another Waterloo.

General Trochu spent yesterday morning with Maître Ducloux, his lawyer, drawing up a will.

The growing antagonism against the emperor has become a real mania both in the army and amongst the public. In fact, the emperor is not recognized any longer now that he has been deprived of his supreme command by the Legislative Body. M. Thiers's influence is growing as the crisis becomes more acute, and he will certainly become the principal member of any future Provisional Government.

The empress is constantly in tears. The officers of the National Guard stationed at the Tuileries, who are invited to the imperial table every day, cannot help noticing the empress's swollen eyes and her lack of appetite. She eats hardly anything.

In army circles there is a growing demand that Marshal Lebœuf and Generals Frossard and de Failly should be court-martialled. General de Failly was surprised and beaten at Beaumont on 30th August, and General Frossard lost the battle of Forbach.

The Government is criticized for announcing a victory between Metz and Verdun, on no better authority than hearsay from passengers arriving in Paris by train from the east. The public is nervously awaiting confirmation.

17th August 1870. The emperor received news during the night of 13th-14th August that the Prussian army, under the command of King William, was marching on Paris by way of Rheims, while the armies of Prince Frederick Charles and the Crown Prince were advancing on the capital by way of Châlons. Prussian advance guards are said to have penetrated the suburbs of Rheims. We shall soon learn if our army intends to engage the enemy in the plains of Champagne or if it will draw back to the fortifications of Paris.

The empress and the ministers, believing that the only way of saving the dynasty is for the emperor to abdicate in favour of his son, have urged Napoleon to send the Prince Imperial back to Paris, but he stubbornly refuses. Indeed, before his departure, the emperor had a lively scene with the empress on this question. He foresaw the danger of leaving his son in Paris, knowing that if he were defeated and the Prince Imperial was at the Tuileries the Government could more easily force him to abdicate. For this reason the emperor took his son with him, and now refuses to let him out of his sight.

The empress is very lonely at the Tuileries. Even the official dignitaries no longer trouble to call on her to offer their sympathy in these moments so critical for the dynasty.

M. Thiers spends long hours in secret conference with General Chabaud-Latour, who has been given the task of defending Paris. Officials at the War Ministry seem more optimistic to-day because of the way Marshal Bazaine has been able to effect his retreat—an operation that is much admired by military strategists. The marshal has doubtless been able to join up with the armies of MacMahon and Trochu at Châlons this morning.

The Bourse was under the influence of this optimism, and closed strong.

18th August 1870. The three successes that Marshal Bazaine has won since 14th August have strengthened the military situation, which, as I pointed out yesterday, was more hopeful. The marshal's retreat is considered a happy stratagem of war.

17th and 18th August were employed by both armies in

burying their dead and removing their wounded. The struggle will shortly be resumed between the united German armies and that of Marshal Bazaine, which has been reinforced by fresh troops from G.H.Q.

The emperor is fading into the background. He and the Prince Imperial, since their departure from Metz, are wandering from Verdun to Châlons and from Châlons to Rheims, no longer taking any part in the military operations, and not daring to return to Paris. Napoleon is like King Lear, driven out of his palace.

M. Louis Veuillot, the great Catholic writer, has been quoting the scriptures in his newspaper, *L'Univers*. He compares Napoleon with Asa, King of Judah, who, having disobeyed God, 'was diseased in his feet, until his disease was exceeding great: yet in his disease he sought not to the Lord but to the physicians. . . .

'And they buried him in his own sepulchres, which he had made for himself in the city of David, and laid him in the bed which was filled with sweet odours and divers kinds of spices prepared by the apothecaries' art; and they made a very great burning for him.'—2 Chronicles xvi.

The emperor was unable to remain at Châlons because of the hostile attitude of the crowd.

The appointment of General Trochu to be Governor of Paris was forced upon the emperor and the empress by the generals. Trochu is an intimate friend of Thiers, and this would suggest that Thiers is assuming an increasingly dominant role which may become similar to that of Talleyrand in 1814.

20th August 1870. The important strategic moves of our army which I outlined to you yesterday are now taking place. The aim of these operations is to smash the Crown Prince's army, which, by following so closely behind Marshal MacMahon's retreat, has been imprudent enough to draw near Chalons by way of Bar-le-Duc. An entire new army has been sent by us to Chalons since 6th August, and there should now be about

Empress Eugénie

General Trochu

150,000 men there, all eager to inflict a resounding vengeance for the defeat of Reichshoffen. If Marshal Bazaine can reach Châlons and make a flank attack against the Crown Prince's army, the Germans might well suffer an important reverse, which would compensate for the disappointment in Paris on 6th August when the victory announced by the Government was found to be untrue. There was delirious joy before the real facts became known.

We are at a critical turning-point.

If we are beaten in this engagement the end of the war will be very near. If, on the other hand, we win in the plains of Châlons, the war will prove to be only in its early stages, for we shall want to carry hostilities into Germany.

The empress keeps a brave face before her ministers, but as soon as they have turned their backs she falls into a terrible state of despondency, and her maternal instincts make her suffer cruelly, for her son is far away and in danger.

I have just heard that Marshal Bazaine's army has been cut off and is besieged in Metz.

22nd August 1870. The communiqué published in the *Journal Officiel* this morning on Marshal Bazaine's position is most disquieting, and suggests that General de Palikao did not tell the whole truth to the Legislative Body on Saturday, 20th August.

Marshal Bazaine is no longer free to operate around Metz, and our only hope is in Marshal MacMahon's new army, which, for some reason we cannot understand, does not yet seem to have moved.

Generals de Palikao and Trochu do not hide their fears of a lightning Prussian thrust at the very gates of Paris. M. Julien Chevreau, Minister of the Interior, complains bitterly of the lack of interest amongst Parisians at so grave a moment, and says that patriotic feeling is much more noticeable in the provinces. The unfortunate Chevreau caught a terrible cold when, at midnight, he drove in an open carriage to the Tuileries for an urgent conference with the empress, who received him in the garden!

The Comtesse Tascher de la Pagerie, suspected of carrying on a treasonable correspondence with high Prussian authorities, has been obliged to go into retirement. Comtesse Walewska and other women of the court are getting ready for a sudden departure.

Members of the revolutionary party in Paris are showing great eagerness to be handed their rifles, not so much to use them against the enemy, but in order to seize power. Palikao and Trochu have decided to keep a close watch on battalions of the National Guard quartered in those parts of Paris where Socialism is specially rampant.

M. Thiers wields a great influence over Gambetta and Ernest Picard.

23rd August 1870. High officials at the War Ministry this morning seem to think that Marshal Bazaine will be able to link up with Marshal MacMahon after all. Bazaine has some 80,000 men, and MacMahon 150,000. This united army should be sufficient to smash the forces of the Crown Prince, who is marching on Paris. Our military strategists suggest, however, that if Bazaine and MacMahon are able to join forces, then the Crown Prince may not come to the walls of Paris but link up with the two German armies before Metz. We should then have to engage the three German armies together.

The Ministry of Foreign Affairs is anxious to point out that Prince Napoleon has gone to Florence on purely personal business.

24th August 1870. It is now five days since Marshal MacMahon started his movement and we ought soon to learn if he has been able to join up with Marshal Bazaine.

The dispatch of M. Nivaghetti to Vienna is the first result of Prince Napoleon's mission to Florence. The idea is not to seek armed help, but simply to save the dynasty.[1] The Cabinet at Florence wants to persuade the Great Powers to discuss preliminary peace terms with the Napoleonic dynasty in order to

[1] In fact the prince went to get armed help, and had specific orders not to entertain the idea of mediation.

prevent a revolution in France. Austria and Russia are said to have agreed to the proposal.

26th August 1870. The Napoleonic party, which fell into the depths of despondency during the early military disasters that overcame the emperor, is lifting its head up again. It is turning its criticism against General Trochu, whom the intimates of the Tuileries and the Palais-Royal accuse of playing the role of Monk, and plotting to reinstate a monarchy. Napoleon's supporters say openly that General Trochu must resign.

M. Emmanuel Arago revealed the vulnerable points in the fortifications of Paris to a Secret Committee yesterday. The committee was composed of 280 members accompanied by an army of stenographers, ushers, and presidential secretaries. The enemy will doubtless have little difficulty in sharing this secret. M. Arago says that the Chamber is one of the disasters of this war. There is now a scheme to elect a small number of deputies who would be in close touch with the ministers, and who could, in confidence, pass on what they are told to their colleagues. This promises some more well-kept secrets!

Because of the imminence of a siege, there is talk of moving the seat of Government, the Senate, and Legislative Body to the provinces. Three cities are named—Blois, Bourges, and Tours.

People who have fled from Montereau, which is twenty-five kilometres from Fontainebleau, claim that Prussian scouts are in sight of the town.

27th August 1870. The only hope for the French army is in the linking up of the armies of Marshals Bazaine and MacMahon.

Two days ago we were of the opinion that MacMahon would be within sight of Bazaine this morning. If this proves the case will they be able to wage battle with success against the two Prussian army corps, considerably strengthened since 18th August? It is significant that King William has thought it safe to detach himself from the main German force to march against Paris with the Crown Prince.

How will Paris defend herself?

The army will doubtless resist heroically.

What of the civilian population?

One already hears rumours that there are certain people willing and even ready to deliver the city to the Germans, and at times this fear of treason from within causes the frightened population to resort to the most extreme acts.

We must be prepared to meet every danger.

Parliamentary circles believe that the emperor plans to take over command of the army again.

'What would you do if the emperor gave an order to Bazaine and Bazaine refused?' somebody asked de Palikao.

'I would back Bazaine,' he answered.

M. Thiers is furious because he has been made a member of the Defence Commission in spite of his refusal. He had told the ministers that he would testify as often as they wished before the commission, but that he would refuse any official nomination. He does not want to owe anything to the present Government. The Napoleonic party hoped to compromise M. Thiers by saying that his refusal showed that he did not want to collaborate in the country's defence. He will make his case clear to-day before the Legislative Body.

There was a violent scene in Secret Committee yesterday. M. Jules Favre accused the Minister of the Interior of treason because he refused to hand out arms to the civilian population.

29th August 1870. It is to-day that General de Palikao is expecting important news from Marshal MacMahon. This is a decisive moment—for us or against us.

General Trochu has at this moment 100,000 men in Paris. Most of these are regular troops, but there are some marines and provincial police. These 100,000 men, together with a section of the Mobile Guard, will man the forts and execute sorties. The National Guard will keep order within the city and occupy the ramparts of the fortifications, and should the Socialists attempt to riot or try to deliver Paris to the Prussians the National Guard will take vigorous action.

The empress, accompanied by General de Palikao and a number of ministers, is getting ready to leave Paris and take up her residence on the other side of the Loire. Her destiny is that of the Empress Marie-Louise. Neither she nor her husband is likely to see Paris again. M. Thiers, General Trochu, and the Legislative Body will become masters of the situation, and will constitute, to some extent, a Provisional Government.

Since the unhappy affair of Mme de la Pagerie, the empress has become extremely reserved. When she is handed a document or a paper she folds it and places it in a pocket without saying a word—such reticence is most unlike her. The accusations of espionage against Mme de la Pagerie are due to the fact that this good lady aims at a pretty wit and political friendships. For some time past she has kept up a corresponcence with several German sovereigns and princes. She certainly spoke freely of everything in letters she sent them, but I doubt if she had any intention of harming her country. Countess Stéphanie kept a diary, in which she noted the most interesting facts of the day and her appreciations of the people she met. She liked to invite her friends to her apartment at the Tuileries and read extracts to them. She wrote with malice and humour.

It has become known that the Crown Prince is not marching on Paris, but is waiting to attack MacMahon before the marshal is able to join up with Bazaine; but MacMahon has at least a day's advance on the Crown Prince, and has cut all the bridges behind him.

A grest and terrible battle is expected on 30th or 31st August.

30th August 1870. The chief concern at the Ministry of War is to discover whether MacMahon will be obliged to engage the Crown Prince alone or whether he can join up with Bazaine, so that our two armies will be united against the three German armies. This battle, which should take place to-day or to-morrow, should prove one of the greatest events of the century.

General Trochu and the Committee of National Defence, backed by M. Thiers, would have preferred a plan whereby all our forces might have been concentrated beneath the walls of Paris and under the fire of our forts. General Palikao, however, agreed with Bazaine and MacMahon. If the operation proves a failure Trochu and the Defence Committee will resort to their plan with what troops can be saved from the Rhine, reinforced by reserves from the provinces.

M. Thiers was present at the meeting of the Defence Council last night, and did not leave until 1 a.m. At 6 a.m. he was on the fortifications.

There is much talk about a letter that Bazaine is supposed to have sent to his wife telling her to be hopeful and to remain at Versailles. Though many important people swore they had read the letter, Mme Bazaine disposed of the matter by saying she had never received it. She is returning to Paris.

Courtiers at the Palais-Royal claim that Princess Clotilde, who, being a daughter of the King of Italy, has royal blood in her veins, is mortified by the fact that her husband, Prince Napoleon, remains at a safe distance from the theatre of war. She has written him a letter full of dignity to remind him that his duty is to shed his blood for France. But Prince Napoleon remains in Florence, and shows no intention of placing his life in danger.

1st September 1870. Marshal MacMahon, having received an order from the emperor to retrace his steps in the direction of the capital to attack the Crown Prince, telegraphed to Paris for instructions. These negotiations wasted twenty-four hours of precious time, and at staff headquarters here there is extreme irritation against the emperor for still aspiring to dabble in military strategy.

It is feared that the bombardment of Strasburg will increase the horrors of the war, and will lead to terrible reprisals.

2nd September 1870. The telegraph cannot fail to tell us very soon the result of the great battle that has been raging in the [department of the] Meuse during the last four days.

MacMahon's retreat on Sedan appears to have been prearranged with Bazaine. Baazine left his retrenchments below

Metz to attack the Prussian army in the rear while MacMahon was turning to attack it in front. MacMahon has received reinforcements of 40,000 men, but we are fighting with a total of only 300,000 against nearly 500,000 Germans. The Prussian dispatches yesterday mentioned that the battle was undecided, which at least proves that King William is not yet claiming victory.

Amongst the National Guard one hears bitter things said against the emperor and the empress. As the emperor is following the army with the baggage, he has been nicknamed 'Baggage III.'

General Trochu is daily becoming more popular.

V. THE REVOLUTION OF 4TH SEPTEMBER

3RD *September 1870.* One must have the courage to face the situation, heart-rending as it is.

We are beaten.

Ever since MacMahon was unable to join up with Bazaine the worst was to be feared.

MacMahon, wounded in the thigh, is doubtless invested in Sedan; Bazaine in Metz.

The Prussian generals will leave sufficient troops in front of these two towns to besiege them. They will then march in force against Paris with all possible speed.

We have no other army ready.

The ex-service men between the ages of twenty-five and thirty-five have not yet been called up, and the 200,000 or 300,000 Mobile Guards are untrained.

How then can we successfully defend Paris against a horde of 400,000 victorious Germans? This is what everybody is asking.

A crisis at home may easily follow the catastrophe to our armies.

Napoleon is ill at a village near the Belgian frontier.

The public does not yet understand the full extent of our disaster, or the perils that beset us. When it does it will rise against the authors of these horrible calamities. The emperor will lose his throne. We are therefore moving towards a Provisional Government.

The various municipal councils have sent telegrams to General Trochu urging him to take the most vigorous measures. He will be forced to assume the powers of a dictator.

5th September 1870. Less than four months ago the Second Empire, by a plebiscite that gave it a majority of 5,800,000 votes, believed itself to be impregnable. We now see it disappear without a single protesting voice.

This regime has fallen even more swiftly than its predecessors.

Louis-Napoleon, who started with one Strasburg, has finished with another. The first did no harm to anybody except himself; this one spells disaster to the entire nation.

The Imperial Government has even been abandoned by the Speaker of the Legislative Body, M. Schneider, the steel magnate of the Creusot works, who, during the final sitting of this Chamber, made a pact with the Left Wing, whose members came up to congratulate him.

Just after 2 p.m. yesterday General de Palikao elbowed his way into the Palais-Bourbon, already invaded by the surging crowd, at the precise moment when M. Schneider was making a speech in praise of Gambetta! The general was so angry that he turned and forced his way out, followed by a small band of deputies of the Right who had timidly returned.

Palikao wanted to proclaim Napoleon IV emperor, with the Empress Eugénie as regent, but Trochu would not hear of it. There has been rivalry between these two men from the beginning.

Prince Orloff, Russian minister at Brussels, known for his pro-French sympathies, is one of the foreign diplomats who have been most actively engaged in trying to obtain intervention by the Great Powers to end the war, but the King of Prussia refuses to treat elsewhere than in Paris.

6th September 1870. The Demagogues and the Socialists of the Internationale are already complaining that they are not represented in the Provisional Government set up at the Hôtel de Ville on 4th September. The party is organizing a policy of agitation that might well bring us back to the days of June 1848. Members of the Republican Government, led by General Trochu and General Le Flô, Minister for War, and backed by Gambetta and Jules Favre, are determined to put down energetically any signs of sedition by the Demagogic party. The epidemic of tree-planting for liberty has started again. Two have just been planted at the Faubourg du Temple and the Place du Château d'Eau.

Deputies of the majority have left Paris for the provinces, where they are to organize a campaign against the Republic.

7th September 1870. As the Prussian army approaches Paris General Trochu hastens the defences of the capital, but he appears to have no illusions, and does not count too much on prolonged resistance.

After our rapid and surprising disasters the defence of Paris is not likely to help us recover from our terrible defeat. It will merely cause more victims.

That is the opinion of our generals, the National Guard, and a large part of the population.

The Government has been unable, with the wreckage of our army, to re-equip more than 80,000 regular troops in Paris. Many of these regiments are tired and demoralized, and would be unable to sustain a long and fierce struggle.

It is difficult to see how, with an army of only 80,000, we can organize sorties against a German force of 400,000. The Prussians have much cavalry, whereas we have none left.

We cannot count on the National Guard, or on the Mobile Guard, which are far from being trained.[1]

---

[1] The National Guard (Garde nationale sédentaire) was the Greek chorus of French revolutions. In 1790 and 1848 it mirrored the noisy shouting of Republicanism. More or less disbanded by Napoleon III during the Second Empire, General de Palikao was obliged to bring it back to life during the Franco-Prussian War. Between 5th and 13th September no fewer than seventy-eight battalions were formed. By a decree of 24th September volunteers could claim payment of 30 sous (about 1*s.* 3*d.*) a day. Workmen from the Red suburbs of Ménilmontant, Charonne, and Belleville joined in a mass, until by December the National Giard boasted 350,000 men. In most of these battalions there was an unhealthy odour of revolution and absinthe. Rowdy manifestations were continually being staged against the Provisional Government, accused of being too *bourgeois.* The National Guard of the siege of Paris might well have played the role of the British Home Guard of 1940. Both were born of the same need. Unfortunately, by its Vigilance Committees, its bombastic debates in smoky cafés under the dim light of oil lamps, and its interminable libations, the National Guard

A National Guard

General Trochu planned to use the fortifications of Paris to keep the enemy busy while we sent another army to attack him from the rear. But we have no army.

The provinces are discouraged by our disasters, and being more Conservative than the capital have no confidence in the Republican Government, composed exclusively of Paris Radicals.

A great national movement is indispensable to save Paris from so great a danger.

The Prussian cavalry will soon cut all communications with Paris by rail, road, and telegraph.

M. Jules Favre, the Minister of Foreign Affairs, shows himself the most courteous of men.

The Bourse to-day was firm on rumours that the United States might mediate, but this American mediation, even if it took place, is not likely to stop the Prussian advance.

8th September 1870. M. Jules Favre was no sooner installed at the Ministry of Foreign Affairs than he appeared surprised not to have received the visits of the Foreign Diplomatic Corps. A person well versed in etiquette pointed out to him that the Foreign Minister first called on the foreign diplomats. M. Jules Favre was very surprised to learn this. Nevertheless, normal etiquette is to be dispensed with and the foreign diplo-

---

paved the way for the Commune. Trochu eventually found his authority menaced by this unwieldy body, for which no definite work was ever found. It was not until the Commune that it sprang into action, having failed to fight the Prussians.

The Mobile Guard was created by a law passed at the beginning of the Franco-Prussian War (10th August 1870). It owed its formation to the preliminary work of Marshal Niel following the critical year of 1866 (Sadowa). The Mobile Guard was not trained, and was ill armed. As in the National Guard, the men elected their officers. Whereas the National Guard was for home duty, the Mobile Guard was a fighting force—often undisciplined, but brave. During the early days of September Mobiles came from all the provinces, and chiefly from Trochu's Brittany. These good Catholics never understood Trochu's patience with the Terrorists. Colonel Douvergne, a battalion commander, once said to Trochu:

'We are 100,000 Mobiles. We could take Paris if we wanted to. Are we not going to Belleville one of these fine mornings to disarm all these miserable fellows?'

mats have agreed to call on M. Favre. He has been warned to cultivate friendly relations with the British ambassador, Lord Lyons, because England and Queen Victoria will play a leading role in the peace negotiations.

M. Jules Favre received the visit of Lord Lyons and several other members of the Foreign Diplomatic Corps yesterday. During the siege of Paris M. Favre and the Diplomatic Corps will take up their headquarters at Tours.

Some 1,500 to 1,800 Mobile Guards are arriving in Paris every day from the provinces.

9th September 1870. The Provisional Government, in hastening to form a National Assembly, shows how anxious it is to shelve, as quickly as possible, the great responsibility it has assumed. Those of us who know the feeling throughout the country are convinced that the majority in the future National Assembly will be Conservative, and will only maintain a Republican framework until the Monarchists have formulated their policy.

One of the first Frenchmen received by M. Jules Favre at the Ministry of Foreign Affairs was General Bocher, whose brother is the estate manager of the royal family of Orleans. During the short stay of the princes in Paris I found that the Prince de Joinville showed a great and profound sorrow for the misfortunes of his country, whereas his nephew, the Duc de Chartres, was fully aware that these misfortunes might serve the cause of the monarchy. The Duc d'Aumale's sentiments were half-way between those of his brother and his nephew.

In M. Thiers's *salon* the opinion is expressed that a monarchy can only be re-established by the head of the Bourbons—the Comte de Chambord.

The elections of officers by members of the National Guard passed off without incident.

M. Victor Hugo treats the Provisional Government with ill humour, and has not called on any of the ministers. The illustrious poet, jealous of Lamartine's role in 1848, expected a Cabinet post in the new Republic.

M. Ulric Fouverolles, a Democrat, called yesterday on M. Jules Favre to complain of the Government's tardiness in dismissing the Napoleonic personnel. M. Jules Favre answered that the first thing was to get rid of the Prussians and that after that there would be plenty of time to distribute positions.

M. Fouverolles left in a huff.

10th September 1870. The delay in the march of the Prussian armies gives us time to complete the defences of Paris, to receive more Mobile Guards from the provinces, to build more redoubts, and to mount guns.

The railroad stations are crowded with families being evacuated to the country.

The wife of a high army officer called on General Trochu to ask whether she should remain in Paris. The general answered that she should leave with all speed, avoid the north coast, and remain, if possible, near a port from which she could embark in case of need. This suggests that General Trochu believes that the invasion may spread beyond Paris. I noticed that when he was talking about the defence of Paris in his *salon* yesterday General Trochu seemed worried and sad.

This morning the Prussians reached Provins (Seine-et-Marne). They are expected to start the siege of Paris on Tuesday or Wednesday at the latest.

At Beauvais, in spite of the energy and bravery of the prefect, the Mobile Guard fled before the Prussians. The military commander at Laon (Aisne) telegraphs that he is at the end of his resources, and will soon be obliged to capitulate. There is a rumour that he has blown up the citadel with all the Prussians who entered it.

There is no truth in any of the mediation talk.

The King of Prussia is becoming more arrogant as he marches towards Paris, and it is at the foot of the walls that he intends to dictate his peace terms.

As soon as the Prussians are in front of Paris all communications will be cut. Do not be surprised, therefore, if you are without news from me for a few days.

13th September 1870. The big review of the National Guard of Paris and the Mobile Guard from the provinces was chiefly notable for the enthusiastic cries of 'Vive Trochu!' Trochu now personifies national defence. The cries of 'Vive la République!' were less numerous and less spontaneous than one would have expected.

The battalions marched off singing the *Marseillaise.* Several sung this refrain:

> 'Bismarck,
> Si tu continues,
> De tous tes Prussiens
> Il n'en restera plus.'

It was easy to see how many people have left Paris. There were hardly any people at the windows.

The 200,000 National Guards and 100,000 Mobiles are determined to resist energetically, and this is all the more to their credit because they are insufficiently trained and ill armed. Some have the Chassepot rifle, others the 'tabatière' rifle, and yet others the 'fusil à piston.' It is to be feared that this difference in types will produce some chaos in the distribution of cartridges. Another danger is in the absence of high command. M. Thiers, in spite of his undoubted qualities, has not the necessary authority to be Commander-in-Chief of these mixed forces.

M. Thiers has left Paris, but he is not very confident about the results of his double mission—to obtain recognition of the Republic by the Great Powers, and to lay the foundations for an honourable peace.

14th September 1870. Diplomats in close touch with the King of Prussia are far from optimistic about our chances to obtain an armistice. The victorious German armies are too near Paris for Bismarck to forgo the satisfaction of signing peace in the capital. We must therefore settle down to a siege.

M. Thiers has been told to find out from the Cabinets in London and St Petersburg exactly what Prussia intends to do with France. I do not know whether M. Thiers will find in London his close friend, Baron de Brunow, the Russian ambassador. The baron is supposed to exercise a great influence over the Emperor Alexander.

Some of our strategists believe that the King of Prussia will not try to take Paris by force of arms, but will try to starve us out.

In order to facilitate peace negotiations there is talk of hastening the elections for the new National Assembly so that we may have a regular Government.

The Foreign Diplomatic Corps sent very favourable telegrams to their Governments yesterday about General Trochu's review of the National Guard and the Mobiles.

The military commander of the little town of Neuf-Brisach (Haut-Rhin) telegraphs that he was attacked yesterday by Prussian scouts, five of whom were taken prisoner. We lost one *chasseur*.

There is bad news from Algiers. The Prefect of Oran wires that there is an insurrection in the south. We have no more troops. It will therefore be necessary to abandon the territory until such time as we can take it back.

15th September 1870. I must point out once again that M. Thiers's mission is not so much to seek an armistice, which the King of Prussia is not willing to grant, as to make the Great Powers understand that it is to their interest not to allow Prussia to impose unbearable conditions on France if Paris is taken.

The Crown Prince has been boasting to some of our officers who have arrived from Sedan that the German army can take Paris in less than a fortnight.

Government circles fear that the Demagogic party will stir up trouble in Paris and in other cities during the siege. This party is master of the municipal councils at Lyons, Marseilles, and Bordeaux. The red flag flies at Lyons, and General Trochu and his colleagues have not yet dared take the necessary measures to uphold the authority of the prefect.

The crisis we are passing through is so acute that one is tempted to quote Louis-Philippe:

'Whatever we do, the unexpected will play the biggest role.'

M. Thiers writes that he is delighted at the reception he is receiving in London, and that Britain is to recognize the new French Government. The Emperor Alexander has authorized Baron de Brunow to tell M. Thiers that he will be happy to receive him.

Prussia's attitude towards Belgium is beginning to annoy the British Government.

VI. THE SIEGE OF PARIS

20TH *September 1870.* I am going to do my very best to dispatch this letter safely to you.

M. Jules Favre is expected back in Paris to-night from Ferrières. He is to make a report on the result of the peace negotiations, but we cannot tell until his return whether King William will have put forward proposals that can be accepted by France.

As soon as M. Jules Favre took over the post of Minister of Foreign Affairs he understood that a beaten France must accept heavy sacrifices to obtain peace. If King William makes this possible the Government of National Defence will accept them in spite of the great uproar of treason that is bound to arise throughout the land.

The occupation by the enemy of the heights of Châtillon makes him master of our forts of Montrouge, Vanves, and Issy, thus exposing all the country south of the ramparts. We needed another week to finish the fort of Montretout, which protects Paris from the west. This has obliged us to abandon this height also. The enemy is therefore in possession of all the heights that dominate our forts. We must now concentrate on the ramparts themselves.

If the King of Prussia makes unacceptable peace terms we shall put up a desperate resistance, causing heavy casualties on both sides.

There was sharp fighting near Saint-Denis until ten o'clock last night, and since six o'clock this morning there have been skirmishes near Charenton, by a corps which is trying to withdraw to Paris.

The dams at Carentan, south of Cherbourg, have been blasted in order to flood the province [of the Manche] and prevent any attack on Cherbourg by land.

I am told that the King of Prussia's ultimatum calls for the cession of Alsace and Lorraine, and a war indemnity of two milliard francs.

21st September 1870. M. Jules Favre is expected some time to-day at the Ministry of Foreign Affairs.

A section of the public would accept Prussian peace terms to put an end to the terrible spilling of blood, in the hope that in two or three years we could make ourselves strong enough for revenge.

But what French Government would dare sign a treaty that abandoned Alsace and Lorraine?

·The Terrorists are busy in Paris. A deputation of fifty officers from the National Guard went to the Ministry of Foreign Affairs yesterday, to state, on behalf of their battalions, that they did not want either an armistice or peace; that they were opposed to general elections, and insist upon a Revolutionary Commune being set up at the Hôtel de Ville which would govern all France.

When this deputation was refused admittance the fifty officers of the National Guard broke down the iron gateway of the ministry, and marched up to M. Jules Ferry, who calmed them by saying that he was not qualified to speak for the whole Government.

The same evening debates were held in all the 'clubs' to decide whether the party should start a Terrorist revolution. These parodists of 1793 are less numerous, less dangerous than those of '48. Meanwhile the Prussian army is preparing to attack our forts.

I have just heard that Jules Favre spent an hour with M. de Bismarck on Monday, two hours on Tuesday, and saw him again this morning. The armistice is now extremely unlikely.

22nd September 1870. By balloon 'Le Neptune' from Montmartre at 7.45 a.m. on 23rd September, landing at Cracomville, near Évreux (Eure), at 11 a.m. 104 kilometres. Aeronaut: Jules Duruof.
Prussia's peace conditions are such that we must fight to the bitter end.

The King of Prussia and M. de Bismarck are no longer content to enter Paris. They are determined to go as far as Bayonne and make the whole country feel the humiliation of foreign invasion.

A new German army of 150,000 men, which is coming by way of Basle, has orders to prevent any French reserves from marching to the help of Paris.

We lack all forms of armament—rifles, guns, and cavalry. Europe remains inactive. Only God can deliver us from the ignominy of being conquered.

The Defence Council believes that we shall be attacked during the next few hours from several points simultaneously.

Although the siege has only been going on for four days the people of Paris are suffering great privations, and we are short of milk and butter. One sees hardly any vegetables in the markets and they are likely to disappear completely during the next few days. Many butchers have closed their shutters, being unable to sell enough to pay their expenses. Judge for yourself what the food situation will be like soon!

There are two things the Government must do urgently—re-establish military discipline, and curb the Terrorist party, which, while accusing its enemies of treason, will be the first to help the Prussians to enter Paris. Victor Hugo and Louis Blanc now show more inclination to align themselves with the Government's policy than Louis-Auguste Blanqui and the other Terrorists. The mass meeting of the Radicals held to-day at the Place de l'Hôtel de Ville passed off quietly.

24th September 1870. By balloon 'La Ville de Florence' from the Boulevard d'Italie at 11 a.m. on 25th September, landing at Vernouillet (Seine-et-Oise) at 3.30 p.m. 30 kilometres. Aeronaut: Gabriel

Garde nationale sédentaire

'Ballon Monté'. A Letter sent out of Paris by Balloon Post during the Siege

Mangin. Since the action at Villejuif yesterday morning, the results of which were much exaggerated by the public, there have only been a few shots exchanged. The Prussian army is massing forces in front of Saint-Denis. We shall soon make a sortie with sufficient troops to hamper the enemy and to destroy some of his preparations for the attack on Saint-Denis.

The Foreign Diplomatic Corps held a meeting yesterday under the presidency of the Papal Nuncio. They decided to remain in Paris until the Prussian generals had, according to custom, given due notice of the bombardment. Several of the ministers at the meeting blamed the precipitation shown by three of the principal ambassadors in leaving the capital. Dr Kern, the Swiss minister, has received his letters accrediting him to the French *Republic*.

The Prussians are unlikely to bombard us till they have taken two or three forts, and they are still a long way from that! We believe they are preparing night attacks.

The National Guard and the Mobiles are beginning to look like soldiers. The Mobile Guard must become our young army, and take the place of the one that has been destroyed.

General Trochu has just been advised that the enemy is placing a battery behind a curtain of trees on the heights of Châtillon. The trees will be felled as soon as the guns are fired.

28th September 1870. By balloon 'Les États-Unis' from La Villette at 10.30 a.m. on 29th September, landing near Mantes (Seine-et-Oise) at 1.30 p.m. 58 kilometres. Aeronaut : Louis Godard. While we are waiting for the big attack, or perhaps I should say the big attacks, of the Prussian army, it is still the Terrorist party that menaces us, and plots in favour of the enemy.

The revolutionary clubs, modelled on those of 1789, are already claiming to govern in the name of the Paris Commune, and red posters bearing this title have been placarded in the city this morning calling upon the National Guards to elect members of the Paris municipality. When this election has taken place you will see a display of armed force to set up the Commune.

It is already functioning at Belleville, the headquarters of the party. The members, at their meeting on 26th September, decided to overthrow the mayor of the XIXth ward and to replace him to-day by an individual of their own choice. This same club has planned the arrest of M. Godillot, a factory owner, and the seizure of his works on the ground of high treason. All this may become serious unless the Government shows a stronger hand in repressing a repetition of the terrorism of 1793. These miserable people alone disturb the admirable spirit which reigns everywhere in Paris—in all parties, amongst all classes.

At G.H.Q. the theory is gaining ground that the Prussians will not attempt to take Paris by storm, but will try to starve us out.

29th September 1870. By balloon 'Le Céleste' from the gas works at Vaugirard at 9.30 a.m. on 30th September, landing at Dreux (Eure-et-Loir) at 11.50 a.m. 81 kilometres. Aeronaut: Gaston Tissandier. Although the newspapers say that the Prussian armies are about to make a vast attack against the city, General Trochu claims that he has definite proof during the last forty-eight hours that the enemy will not attack Paris. The plan of campaign drawn up by Bismarck at Versailles is to starve us. The Prussian army will occupy the strategic positions round the capital, and prevent any help from reaching us from the provinces. Bismarck believes that Parisians will not stand a siege for more than a week.

The Terrorist party is doing everything it can to help M. de Bismarck. Ledru-Rollin, who kept very quiet during the first days of the siege, is now taking charge of the movement to set up a revolutionary Commune in Paris. He made a speech to the club of the VIIth ward yesterday announcing his decision. The Government is growing weaker as the Terrorist party becomes bolder. Ministers close their eyes to the danger, preferring to play for time, not realizing that they will be the first to be swept from power.

30th September and 1st October 1870. The Prussian army has remained on the defensive since 23rd September, fortifying its positions to the east, south-east, and north of Paris. This confirms what I told you yesterday about Bismarck's plan of campaign. To counter this we shall be obliged to increase the offensive we started yesterday. Ex-service men and good marksmen will be taken from the ranks of the National Guard, but we shall not make large sorties until we hear of the approach of our army of the Loire. For the time being our offensive will merely consist in retaking Choisy-le-Roi in order to free the Orleans and Lyons railroad line, and make a safe passage for our relief army.

The Ministers of the Interior and Education are busy revising the pensions given by Napoleon to some of our writers. Théophile Gautier and Ernest Feydeau had a grant of 3,000 francs a year. M. Octave Feuillet, who is immensely rich from his plays and novels, was given a lucrative post as librarian of an imperial château.

The emperor gave a splendid house in the Avenue Friedland to his mistress, Marguerite Bellanger. The rich furnishings were taken away prior to 4th September, but the house has now been requisitioned by the Mayor of Paris for evacuees from Puteaux.

3rd October 1870. General Trochu knows that he cannot, in face of the Prussian defensive plan, remain inactive for ever. This would play right into the hands of Bismarck. Nevertheless our last sortie of 29th September has shown that we must, in future, operate with much larger forces, both in men and in materials.

Two post office employees who left Paris by balloon have been able to return through the enemy lines. They say that the Prussians cover an immense territory, and that their lines are close enough to come quickly to each other's aid.

Our National Guard will provide 100,000 young men. They will be equipped with Chassepots and Remingtons. The Mobile Guard now has 125,000 trained men, some of whom have already been under fire. We could certainly muster 80,000 ex-service men in Paris, including the *gendarmes*, the Republican Guard, the Marines, and the customs officials. This total gives us more than 300,000 men within the walls of the city, who will soon be able to attack the Prussian army.

The army of the Loire, which is coming to our aid, is at least 150,000 strong, so that there is no reason why we should not beat the Prussians.

Munition factories in Paris, at Bourges, Douai, Indret, and Toulouse, are turning out a considerable quantity of cannon and mitrailleuses.

Military leadership is what is most lacking. This will come because France cannot perish.

General Burnside, an American, has come back from Ferrières with a note for M. Jules Favre from M. de Bismarck, containing fresh peace conditions, less stringent than the last. After consulting his colleagues M. Favre will answer this note to-night.

4th October 1870. The Terrorist party has begun to attack General Trochu in the Radical press and in the clubs.

Victor Hugo has asked Gustave Flourens to let him know when the Belleville battalion of the National Guard makes a sortie. Victor Hugo says he would like to accompany it, but without being armed, for, he says: 'I am of those who die but do not kill.'

6th October 1870. By balloon ' Armand Barbès' leaving Montmartre at 11 a.m. on 7th October with Gambetta and Spuller, landing at Montdidier (Somme) at 3.30 p.m. 98 kilometres. Aeronaut: Trichet. I continue to make use of the balloon post at each of its departures without knowing if my letters reach you. No letters have arrived in Paris from outside since 28th September. The public is getting depressed by the length of the siege, and by our apparent inability to take the offensive. General Trochu believes in being extremely prudent.

I am afraid that our regular troops number no more than 60,000, and the morale is not always as good as it might be. They are still under the influence of our military reverses.

A sailor guarding a fort during the siege of Paris —a contemporary drawing

There are several excellent battalions of the Mobiles which can be of great use in future sorties, but the majority have not yet acquired the necessary training, and they will have to be equipped with artillery before they move to the attack. These shortcomings are even more marked in the National Guard, which would be literally butchered if sent against the Germans, and then the Anarchists would not fail to cry treason. General Trochu points out that the Prussians are drawn up in such a way that they can bring 200,000 men to any given point within two or three hours.

Help from the provincial armies becomes increasingly problematical.

The Terrorists at Lyons have just prevented the departure of 40,000 regular troops assembled in that city who were to join up with the army of the Loire, and, what is more, the Terrorist party is trying to make the army adopt the red flag, which it has refused to do.

A committee of war ideas has adopted a new invention by which burning oil can be sprayed over 300 yards from a hose. It will be used on the ramparts.

Every postman who accompanies the mail by balloon will receive 1,000 francs.

The public seems satisfied, on the whole, by a decree forbidding the National Guard to hold armed demonstrations.

7th October 1870. The Government has just been warned that the Terrorists are preparing to attack the Hôtel de Ville. The building is to be taken over by National Guardsmen who are members of the party. The idea is to proclaim the Paris Commune, which is another word for the Commune of Belleville, which believes it ought to govern not only Paris, but the whole of France.

This may sound very droll, but the movement will become dangerous if it is not checked. The party is made up of some 12,000 vagabonds, capable of anything.

General Trochu sent for a number of battalion commanders

La Cantinière

of the Provincial National Guard to ask if he could count on them if the Government were attacked. Some gave satisfactory answers; others said they had come to fight the Prussians, but could not answer for the reactions of their men if told to fire on Frenchmen.

This is the crisis that Bismarck has been counting on, but the danger is less than it was in June 1848, and the Government can become master of the situation if it is willing to act.

There was a sharp cannonade between 11 a.m. and noon to-day from the forts of Montrouge and Vanves. It looks as if the enemy may attack.

8th October 1870. Because of the balloon post I have to use such thin paper that the writing is extremely hard to read. I suggest you place my letter over an ordinary sheet of white paper to help you decipher it.

Most Parisians were glad to read in the *Journal Officiel* this morning that the Government has decided to defy the Terrorists and cancel the municipal elections.

This note appears on the day following the departure of M. Gambetta. M. Gambetta's journey is not merely to stir up enthusiasm in the provinces, as the newspapers suggest. Some of his supporters in the Radical party made it difficult for him to pursue a strong policy, and this was a handicap not only to himself, but to the Government. M. Gambetta was glad to leave, and the Government, backed by the great majority of the country, will now be able to oppose the provocations of the Terrorist party.

The military attaché of the St Petersburg Cabinet has reached Tours to hand over his report on conditions in Paris. This will be immediately dispatched to Russia. So far St Petersburg has been relying on the reports of its military attaché with the Prussian army, and these reports are obviously written from the German viewpoint. As soon as the Russian military attaché in Paris has delivered his report to his ambassador at Tours, he will return to the capital, travelling through the Prussian lines.

The Terrorist party has just sent 3,000 of its supporters to the Place de l'Hôtel de Ville to shout: 'Vive la Commune!' and 'A bas les réactionnaires!' A battalion of the National Guard is posted in front of the Hôtel de Ville. Drums are being sounded to call up all the National Guard. Meanwhile the guns of Mont-Valérien thunder against the Prussians.

10th October 1870. The slowness and indecision of General Trochu's military campaign are due to the fact that everything was planned for passive resistance. When the Prussians, instead of attacking us, put themselves on the defensive, all General Trochu's plans had to be changed. This takes a long time.

Troops must be trained and war material produced. Thanks to the enthusiasm in our factories and the help we are being sent from the provinces, this work is proceeding rapidly.

Important operations are to start to-day. A regiment of Zouaves, several regiments of infantry, and a number of battalions of Mobile Guards, with some artillery, have been moved to Neuilly and Courbevoie.

A Prussian army corps of 80,000 men is on the right bank of the Loire to intercept our relief army. The provinces must hurry to our help, for, according to prisoners we have taken, the Prussians expect to receive all their heavy artillery for attacking our forts and bombarding Paris by the end of the week.

King William's staff intends to employ considerable forces against Mont-Valérien, which impedes them.

None of the pigeons taken by M. Gambetta in his balloon has yet returned, and at the Ministry of the Interior there is a good deal of anxiety about the minister's safe arrival.

Mont-Valérien, the fort of Issy, and the guns on the Seine are to bombard Saint-Cloud in an attempt to dislodge the Prussians.

The château of Saint-Cloud, so full of historic gems, will be destroyed.

11th October 1870. By balloon 'Washington' from the Gare d'Orléans at 8.30 a.m. on 12th October, arriving Cambrai (Nord) at 11.30 a.m.

204 kilometres. Aeronaut: Albert Bertaux. We are waiting to hear the result of the operations outside Paris.

A telegram from Gambetta announces that the provinces are rising *en masse*, especially Brittany. It appears that all the men between the ages of twenty and fifty are marching to our aid, accompanied by the doctors of each district and the priests of each parish. The rich landowners of Brittany and the local councils have imported Remington rifles from England. The commanders of Mobile Guard battalions of Brittany have told General Trochu that as long as he remains at the head of the Government they will be responsible for peace in the capital. The Communists of Belleville would do well to take this into account.

A Republican farming expert is to organize the production of vegetables in Paris allotments.

12th October 1870. A special meeting of the Government and the Council of Defence was held yesterday. General Trochu, without going into details, stated that important military operations were being carried out by the army of Paris. Six new machine-guns were presented to the Government and the Defence Council. The general also gave some information about the output of cannon. The War Ministry is taking special measures to guard Mont-Valérien, believing that the enemy, unable to take this fortress, will attempt to tunnel beneath it and blow it up.

Several battalions of the National Guard have been warned that they will be called upon to serve outside the ramparts.

A balloon left the Gare d'Orléans at seven o'clock this morning carrying six delegates to stir up enthusiasm in the provinces.

Meat is rationed from to-day. Gas is to be rationed shortly, and there are already hardly any gas lamps lighted in the streets after midnight.

13th October 1870. By balloon 'Le Godefroy Cavaignac' from the Gare d'Orléans at 9.45 a.m. on 14th October, arriving Brillon (Meuse) at 2.45 p.m. 257 kilometres. Aeronaut: Godard père. The public is convinced that the Comte de Chambord and the princes of the house of Orleans are at the head of the relief armies now marching towards Paris. It is said that the princes have asked the delegation of Tours to give them back their privileges, taken away by the emperor.

Kings do not ask permission. They act!

It is only natural that members of the house of Bourbon, to whom France owes its glory, should wish to fight.

Their presence in the army cannot possibly hamper the National Defence Government, still less overthrow it. The nation will have time after the war to decide on its form of government.

Prussian infiltrations have appeared in the department of the Sarthe.

M. de Kératry, who is to leave Paris on a diplomatic mission, will first go to one of our ports, where he is to take delivery of a consignment of British and American rifles to the value of 75,000,000 francs. M. de Kératry resigned from his post of Prefect of Police because he was disgusted by the denunciations he received every day from members of the Government against their own colleagues!

General Burnside tells his friends that M. de Bismarck seems disappointed at not being able to enter Paris. The American general during his second visit brought no British newspapers, having been asked not to do so by M. de Bismarck. He took none of our papers back to the Prussian camp.

Since early morning there is brisk fighting by our troops trying to reach Choisy-le-Roi. Mont-Valérien is firing to cause a diversion.

14th October 1870. By balloon 'Christophe-Colomb' from the Gare d'Orléans at 1.15 p.m., arriving Montpothier (Aube) at 5 p.m. 114 kilometres. Aeronaut: Albert Tissandier. The engagement yesterday was nothing more than a repetition of the one on 29th September, and obtained no better result.

That is to say that what General Trochu calls 'offensive reconnaissance' is merely an unsuccessful attempt to occupy Boqueux and Châtillon.

This is our present situation.

The Prussians are unable to enter Paris, but we cannot dislodge them.

General Trochu says we must wait until the end of the month to see if the provincial armies come to our help.

According to General Burnside no second call-up has taken place in Germany. Her soldiers, at the walls of Paris, are mostly under thirty-two years of age. The older men are still in Germany and, because Prussia has now nothing to fear from Austria, 80,000 Bavarian troops who were on the frontier have now been drafted to positions near Paris.

M. de Kératry left to-day in the balloon *Godefroy-Cavaignac*.

Last night he had a long interview with Henri Rochefort, who said:

'I am dissatisfied with my colleagues in the Defence Committee. They are all at sixes and sevens, and argue interminably about trifles. The business of the country is suffering. I am very much afraid of a German victory, and if I am right the only thing left for me will be to go back and edit the *Lanterne*.'

On the other hand, Henri Rochefort's colleagues accuse *him* of making trouble. They say that discussions in the Defence Committee become bitter as soon as he takes part in them.

Ledru-Rollin is no longer on speaking terms with Charles Delescluze, editor of the Red newspaper *Le Réveil*, because he refuses to go on with the party's campaign for municipal elections.

The moderate Liberals are opening a political club on Monday evening at the Porte Saint-Martin theatre.

In 1848 we had a club called 'La Vésuvienne'—a political association formed by ladies of easy virtue. Our Republic of 1870 has produced the 'Amazones'!

15th October 1870. By balloon 'Jules Favre N° 1' from the Gare d'Orléans at 7.20 a.m. on 16th October, arriving Foix de Chapelle (Belgium) at 12.20 p.m. 298 kilometres. Aeronaut: Louis Godard jeune. General Trochu's report this morning confirms the news I sent you over a week ago—that the Government of Paris would not willingly send masses of untrained National Guards and Mobiles to be butchered by the Prussians.

The relief armies from the provinces must come quickly, however, for we are running short of beef and mutton. The present rations give only a very small amount of meat to each family every three days. A business man has told the Government he will bring 80,000 head of cattle and 100,000 sheep into Paris if the blockade can be raised to free one railroad terminus for forty-eight hours. But that is precisely the difficulty.

The Prussians show an insolent faith in victory. A Prussian colonel exclaimed arrogantly to one of the heads of the Swiss ambulance corps after the engagement at Châtillon:

'Why don't you persuade the French to stop this war? They are spilling blood to no purpose, for we have ten army corps, and they can't help being beaten.'

17th October 1870. By balloon 'Victor Hugo' from the Jardin des Tuileries at 11.45 a.m. on 18th October, arriving at Vaubéron (Aisne) at 5.30 p.m. 117 kilometres. Aeronaut: Nadal. General Trochu, in spite of his report, has been obliged by public opinion to mobilize the National Guard and announce a coming offensive. Some 40,000 are expected to volunteer and these, together with the regular army and the Mobile Guards, should make a total of 200,000 for the offensive. An artillery regiment left the capital this morning with its field equipment.

The *Journal Officiel* has not yet announced the safe arrival of M. de Kératry. There are fears that his balloon may have fallen in the enemy's lines.

The confidence expressed by M. Thiers in his last report is not shared by all the members of the Government. M. Ernest Picard was asked yesterday what he knew about the military situation in the provinces.

'I am afraid,' he answered, 'that the men who are raising our relief armies will arrive too late to save us.'

'But these men are party men; we should show them consideration,' said his friend.

'I don't care what they are,' snapped the Minister of Finance, 'as long as they get here!'

M. Picard added that personally he would not be hostile to an Orleanist revival.

24th October 1870. The Government hopes we shall be masters of Choisy-le-Roi, which would allow traffic to run into the Gare d'Orléans, and possibly also into the Gare de Lyon. The idea is to free these two railroad termini just as the army of the Loire arrives in sight. I know one high Government official who is so certain that we shall free one or both of these stations that he is making plans to send his wife away to the country because, he says, the 'air of Paris no longer suits her.'

The Government believes that the Prussians have an army of 150,000 men, which operates in the region of the Loire, while another 300,000 remain in front of Paris.

One-third of the National Guard has failed to provide any volunteers for the mobilization. On the other hand some battalions have given more than the quota of 150 asked for, with the result that we should have a total of at least 40,000 for active service outside the ramparts.

M. de Sauley, a retired artillery officer, whose wife was a lady-in-waiting to the ex-empress, is anxious to become a captain of artillery in the National Guard, but it appears that his request will be refused because the gunners of this regiment will not appoint the husband of an ex-lady-in-waiting as an officer.

To give some idea of the alacrity with which Parisians would flock to places of entertainment if these were reopened, one had only to see the huge crowd that went to the Cirque yesterday to hear a concert of classical music. Many people were unable to find seats. A famous Catholic orator, Abbé Duquesnay, priest of Saint-Laurent, was cheered enthusiastically when he spoke.

His warm reception by a crowd of nearly 6,000 people was in
strong contrast with the anti-religious campaign now being
waged by so many Paris mayors.

Although the siege has now lasted thirty days, Paris has not
suffered any serious privation. One is struck by the calm, the
courage, and the patience of the population.

The meat ration is now two ounces a day.

25th October 1870. M. Rampon, Director-General of the Forts,
spoke last evening to a postman who succeeded in crossing the
Prussian lines. This unfortunate fellow was surprised by the
Germans on the nineteenth. His telegrams and letters were
seized, and he was thrown into a dungeon, where his guard told
him he was to be shot. It was only yesterday morning that he
was released, on the promise that he would never try to cross
the lines again. He was led blindfold to the gates of Paris.
The poor devil was made to climb up and down so many steps
and barked his shins against so many stones that he is convinced
that the Prussians have built the most solid fortifications. He
came from Tours. It may well be that his imprisonment by the
enemy, and the rough time he had there, added to his pessimism,
but he declares that the movement in the provinces lacks enthusiasm, that it is most unlikely that the relief armies will reach
us in time, and that the feeling in Tours is that we shall be beaten
by famine.

M. Ernest Picard, Minister of Finance, is also a defeatist, and
is often in disagreement with his colleagues. The Government
would like to send him to Tours to get him out of the way, but
as he is very fat he would need a very large balloon! M. Jules
Ferry [Mayor of Paris and Prefect of the Seine] is also supposed
to be leaving shortly. The more optimistic members of the
Government believe that the blockade can be raised from Paris
within a fortnight.

*26th October 1870. By balloon 'Vauban' from the Gare d'Orléans
at 9 a.m. on 27th October, arriving Commercy (Meuse) at 1 p.m.
370 kilometres. Aeronaut: Guillaume.* M. Jules Favre is busy

drawing up a new answer to M. de Bismarck, and another one for the Great Powers. This last note is based on observations made by M. Thiers during his sojourn in London, Vienna, and St Petersburg, and contained in a telegram which reached Paris three days ago.

The eleventh Government publication containing the secret papers of the family of Napoleon III is held up because M. Jules Favre, to whom the proofs were sent, is afraid that their publication might annoy the imperial family! The collection contains letters exchanged between the emperor and several crowned heads of Europe, which are full of interesting disclosures.

27th October 1870. Preparations for a great offensive that is to raise the blockade of Paris are now well advanced.

Our delegates in Tours have wired that two relief armies are at last on the move. One army is coming from the centre, and the other from the north. These include three divisions brought back from Algeria, 10,000 Turcos, three squadrons of Spahis, and 20,000 sailors under the command of Admiral Fourichon.

An entrenched camp of 60,000 men protects Bourges, where the enemy is anxious to blow up the arsenal.

We may therefore expect big news during the early days of November. Impatient critics continue to attack General Trochu, saying that he ought to sacrifice 10,000 men to save Paris.

The War Ministry has just bought 6,000 horses to draw 600 gun carriages.

Many private people and every Government department are raising funds to buy cannon, each of which will bear the name of the person or the department that has given it. The telegraph section of the Post Office will call its cannon 'The Telegraph,' and on it will be engraved the words:

'Not an inch of territory,
Nor a stone from our fortresses.'

The number of foreigners leaving Paris increases every day.

Many Portuguese left yesterday. Dr Kern, the Swiss minister, has sent M. de Bismarck a list of his nationals who want to return to Switzerland. They will be given safe-conducts across the Prussian lines. The American colony leaves on Friday, but both Mr Washburne, the American minister, and Dr Kern will stay in Paris.

28th October 1870. By balloon 'Colonel Charras' from the Gare du Nord at midday on 29th October, arriving Montigny-le-Roi (Haute-Marne) at 5 p.m. 308 kilometres. Aeronaut: Gilles. Paris is in a state of intense agitation following a statement by Félix Pyat in his newspaper *Le Combat* last night that Marshal Bazaine has capitulated at Metz.

At 11 p.m. yesterday, in spite of the complete darkness in which the boulevards are plunged during the siege, groups of people were excitedly discussing the possibility of this news being true.

Félix Pyat, successful playwright but embittered Communist, has been writing inflamed articles. His paper, *Le Combat*, is one of the three chief newspapers of the Red party, the other two being *Le Reveil*, belonging to Charles Delescluze, and the *Patrie en Danger*, belonging to Blanqui.

Some people accuse Pyat of trying to cause a panic. They point out that the Communist writers began by exploiting the question of municipal elections. Then they decided to make friction amongst the members of the National Guard, for, as soon as General Trochu announced that he would not send the National Guard outside the walls of Paris to fight the Prussians, these writers claimed that the Government was afraid to hand out rifles to the populace. When General Trochu announced he would mobilize the National Guard, these same writers yelled that he was scheming to send brave democrats to their death.

31st October 1870. By balloon 'Fulton' from the Gare d'Orléans at 8.45 a.m. on 2nd November, arriving Cossé (Maine et Loire) at 5 p.m. 345 kilometres. Aeronaut: Le Gloënnec. Paris, already saddened last evening by the recapture by the Prussians of Le Bourget, a reverse that could have been avoided with more foresight, woke up in consternation this morning when the news was confirmed that Marshal Bazaine had capitulated at Metz.

M. Thiers, since his return to Paris, has given a detailed account of his journey to members of the National Defence Committee.

He says that the three Great Powers (England, Russia, and Austria) are watching with some anxiety the Prussian victories, and the crumbling of French resistance, but they believe that it is too late for us to recoup our losses, and that we must be prepared to accept great sacrifices.

M. Thiers adds that we must not count on any foreign help, and that it would be also idle for us to expect much support from the provinces because the politicians and prefects whom we sent to stir up enthusiasm, far from occupying themselves exclusively with patriotic ardour, are plunged in party politics, and have alienated the rural districts by their vociferations against the priests and the pope.

M. Thiers sums up by saying that we should convene the Constituent Assembly at the earliest moment to lay the foundations for an armistice.

In Paris, however, the Anarchist party will not hear of an armistice, and wants to seize the opportunity of overthrowing the Government and setting up the Commune. We are approaching another crisis.

A huge crowd gathered outside the Hôtel de Ville at 1 p.m. to-day. Several battalions of the National Guard arrived. They were led by military bands and shouted:

'We don't want an armistice!' 'We shall fight to the death!'

At 3 p.m. a shot was fired, and the crowd showed signs of panic.

M. Thiers is leaving for Versailles this evening to confer with Bismarck.

2nd November 1870. The Government is once again being

blamed for its weakness. Though it has dismissed nine insurrectionary battalion commanders, no measures have been taken against the leaders of the movement.

Only one of the four decrees published in the *Journal Officiel* this morning is signed by Henri Rochefort. There is a rumour that he will be obliged to resign because of revelations at the Hôtel de Ville that he divulged the news about the fall of Metz to Félix Pyat. Pyat and Gustave Flourens [Communard son of a famous physiologist] had promised to lie about the source of their information. All this is not saying very much for our rulers.

Étienne Arago [Mayor of Paris and brother of the distinguished scientist] is in trouble too. He and his deputies who tried to juggle with the municipal elections have been asked to resign, but M. Arago does not want to resign, and he will doubtless end by winning the day.

I visited the Hôtel de Ville this morning. Some damage has been caused by the hooligans who tried to take it by storm the other day. The council chamber has been partly wrecked, and the magnificent plan of Paris, one of the artistic treasures of the building, has been defaced. The curtains were cut about, and a fine Louis XV *canapé* smashed. Many small *objets d'art* were stolen. A few demonstrators broke down the door leading to the telegraph room, but the employees prevented them from doing much damage to the instruments.

Gambetta's secretary negotiated the 200,000,000-franc loan at 44 in London. There is much talk at Tours about the scandalous commissions made by certain politicians on this floatation.

4th November 1870. By balloon 'Ville de Châteaudun' from the Gare du Nord at 9.45 a.m. on 6th November, arriving Réclainville (Eure-et-Loir) at 5 p.m. 106 kilometres. Aeronaut: Bosc. A number of battalion commanders of the National Guard called on General Trochu this morning to insist that the Government should defend the nation not only from external, but also from internal enemies. General Trochu gave a solemn promise to this effect. We shall see if he intends to keep it.

The Prussians are very active near Le Bourget and Drancy. These two villages are just beyond La Villette, which is a Red stronghold. Does the enemy think that this will help him pierce our defences?

7th November 1870. When, a few days ago, it became known in Paris that peace discussions were going on, many inflamed speeches were made by orators who said that it was treason not to continue the war.

Now that an armistice is refused the is a wave of despondency.

People who own stocks of food, and who have a little money, are not yet feeling the siege too badly.

There is, however, great hardship amongst the poorer people. These can no longer afford to buy the very small meat ration allotted to them because prices have not been controlled and are rising each day. Vegetables have reached prohibitive values.

Many families are near starvation, and their physical resistance is sapped. Mothers have no milk for their babies, and the infant mortality is rising.

I know of one woman whose small child is being breast-fed by a kindly neighbour, but this woman in turn is growing weaker every day, and her own babies will soon die.

General Trochu and our military chiefs do not hide their fears that we have small chance of success, but they will not fail to make a supreme effort to save their honour.

As the mobilization of the National Guard has not yet been organized, we can only count on the regular army and the Mobiles—scarcely 100,000 men really capable of standing up to the Germans who, since the capitulation of Metz, number anything between 350,000 and 500,000.

M. Thiers, during his conferences with M. de Bismarck, tried to make him understand that the successive capitulations at Sedan, Strasburg, and Metz have reduced France so much that it would be a wise policy for Prussia to be generous in victory, instead of being so uncompromising that the French nation might nurse vengeance for generations to come.

M. Thiers said that the German refusal to allow food to be sent to Paris was all the more unreasonable because the new Assembly which is to be elected during the armistice would certainly be disposed to agree to heavy sacrifices for peace, the provinces being even more anxious than Paris to see the war at an end.

9th November 1870. Political discussion is exclusively centred on the possibility of an armistice, and we are anxiously waiting for news from M. Thiers, who is in conference at Versailles with M. de Bismarck.

The negotiations are taking longer than was expected. It looks as if unexpected difficulties had arisen.

M. Jules Favre stated in a proclamation yesterday that the Government is still determined not to give up an inch of our territory, but he no longer adds the familiar words 'nor a stone from our fortresses.' This suggests that the Government is leaving the door open for concessions.

Our strategists point out that even before the war General Trochu was against fortified cities as essential bulwarks on our frontier. If, therefore, he agreed to the dismantling of Strasburg and Metz he would only remain true to his oft-repeated views!

In the event of an armistice the Government is fully prepared for a terrible outcry from the Jacobins [1] and Communists.

12th November 1870. The Ministry of Foreign Affairs has received news of what happened at Versailles on Thursday evening.

While M. de Bismarck and a number of foreign observers were discussing with M. Thiers the groundwork for an armistice, the King of Prussia sent a message to Bismarck asking that the conference should be continued in the royal presence. The

---

[1] The Club des Jacobins was a famous club in the French Revolution. It met in the Convent of the Jacobins in the rue Saint-Honoré. Its members were amongst the most exalted of the Revolutionaries. The club was dissolved in 1799. At this period the word was revived to denote the more violent democrats.

delegates were then taken to see the king, who kept on inter-rupting the discussions to say how anxious he was for peace.

This morning the Paris newspapers all came out with the news that an armistice was signed, but this statement is premature. The members of our Government are divided on the question, some of them urging immediate peace, others saying that we should try our luck again, adding that the only way of not signing a dishonourable peace is by obtaining some quick success against the Prussians. The war party points out that we have now as many guns and mitrailleuses as the enemy, and that they are probably of better quality and wider range. If we put all our artillery in the field we might see the fortune of war turn in our favour.

The Minister of Public Works, who heads the war party, points out that a very large section of the public accuses the Govern-ment of cowardice. He insists that we should put our army into the field.

Those who want peace argue that the Prussians now occupy all the vantage points, that our army is disheartened, and that if we are beaten in a final gamble the Germans will seize all our war material, our fleet, and occupy the whole of France.

'It is much more prudent,' they say, 'to accept the Prussian armistice now.'

The Defence Council broke up without reaching a decision.

The officers in charge of the forts called on General Trochu yesterday, to tell him that they are willing to allow the National Guard to serve on the ramparts, but that they do not want them in the forts.

14th November 1870. The Great Powers are still discussing an armistice, but General Trochu's proclamation to-day shows that the war party has the upper hand in the Government.

It is clear, from his proclamation, that General Trochu has given up hope of receiving any help from the provincial armies, but that he is willing to put all our forces into the field for a final battle. Unfortunately the general is pessimistic in advance.

He makes no effort to conceal his personal view that this final effort is doomed to failure, and he adds that he must have at least ten or twelve days to make his military preparations.

During the next ten days the four neutral Powers will send their views on an armistice to Versailles.

The military plans that General Trochu is obliging his colleagues to adopt do not meet with the approval of the other generals in the army of Paris.

General Trochu has quarrelled with General Vinoy, which is unfortunate, because General Vinoy is the only military commander to have scored any victories over the enemy since the beginning of the siege. In spite of his successes General Vinoy was, until recently, merely in command of an army corps. This was so obviously an injustice that he has now been placed in charge of the Third Army.

The Government has decided to take no action against the ringleaders of the attack on the Hôtel de Ville. It is now revealed that the Government made a bargain with these men, promising them immunity if they would capitulate. As a result of this M. Edmond Adam, Prefect of Police, resigned, but Ernest Cresson, his successor, who arrested the ringleaders, says that *he* will resign if they are released!

All this is deplorable because we have never been in greater need of a strong Government.

15th November 1870. The success of one of our relief armies at Orleans has been greeted with great satisfaction by Parisians, not so much because of its military importance, but because it proves the existence of provincial support. We must follow up this success. The Prussians never fail to bring up considerable forces to recapture a lost position, and so the Government is trying to discover whether General d'Aurelle de Paladines is in a position to face increased pressure.

General Trochu intends to take control of the great military offensive he has drawn up, and as he is an ardent Catholic he has taken the precaution of confessing to a priest.

It is rumoured that the Admiral de La Roncière will be Governor of Paris during General Trochu's absence at the front, and if this proves the case the Jacobins would be wise to keep quiet because the admiral does not stand any nonsense.

Over 40,000 men of the army of the Loire are marching to the help of General d'Aurelle de Paladine's army corps, so that he may have sufficient reinforcements to face the Prussian counter-attack.

Meanwhile a part of the German army from Metz has passed through Dijon on its way to Lyons.

16th November 1870. Preparations are well advanced for the great offensive to raise the siege. A special railroad track has been built to carry the big guns destined to pound one of the strongest Prussian positions. Orders have been issued to the railroad companies to keep their locomotives under pressure, and to have their rolling stock ready for immediate use. The Telegraph Company has recruited employees to work a control system between the various armies. Even the generals who a few days ago were reluctant to collaborate with General Trochu are now enthusiastic about his scheme.

General Trochu sent one of his aides-de-camp out of Paris by balloon during the night with verbal instructions for the commanders of our relief armies.

A War Council was held this morning. General Trochu's plans were carried unanimously by the ministers, the generals, and the admirals. The campaign must begin quickly, because the Prussians are themselves getting ready.

18th November 1870. The Ministry of Foreign Affairs understands that the report of the four neutral Powers on the armistice has reached Versailles and that a meeting is to be held there to-day or to-morrow, at which Prussia will draw up an answer. We should therefore know within a few days what King William and M. de Bismarck have decided.

The War Ministry is busy mounting the new gun batteries, but several generals are criticizing General Trochu for having divulged his plans for an offensive so long in advance. As several people are now in the secret there is every reason to fear indiscretions which may turn to treason. The Prussians, who have known for at least a week that something is in the air, have already had ample time to take their precautions. It is feared, for instance, that the Prussian army corps from Metz, which was on its way to Lyons, may have been ordered to return to Orleans to cut off the army of the Loire.

Several battalions of the National Guard are enthusiastic. Others are very slack, and more and more men are seeking exemption. General Thomas reviewed a number of these battalions yesterday, and was struck by their indifference.

He has given orders for a volunteer battalion from Menilmontant to be discharged. It was made up of young fellows under eighteen years old, most of whom suffered from rickets or under-nourishment.

A deputation from the National Guard of Belleville called on General Thomas to complain that married men were being called up. General Thomas answered that after clamouring so loudly for rifles the Guard must now use them against the Prussians. These fiery Communists from Belleville are not keen to meet the enemy.

The balloons that left Paris on 4th and 12th November fell into the German lines and my letters carried by them will therefore not reach you.[1]

21st November 1870. As Prussia persists in refusing any armistice we are obliged to rely on a military victory.

General Trochu is preparing night and day for his great offensive, but his plans seem far from ready.

It will take at least ten days to equip the army and the National Guard. The Paris Cab Company can no longer feed its 8,000

[1] *Galilée*, which left Paris at 2 p.m. on 4th November, landed near Chartres, and was captured by the Prussians, but *Ferdinand Flocon*, which left Paris at 9 a.m., made a safe journey.

Daguerre, which left Paris at 9 a.m. on 12th November, fell into Prussian hands at Jossigny. One mailbag was thrown overboard and rescued by a woodman at Ferrières.

horses because of the rise in the price of oats. It therefore offered to sell 1,500 horses to the Ministry of War, but though the offer has been accepted the ministry says that it does not want delivery before the second week in December.

This suggests that the offensive is unlikely to take place before then.

27th November 1870. Several army corps taking part in the coming offensive have already taken up positions, and have enough food for six days.

The National Guard will man the forts and act as a reserve.

29th November 1870. By balloon 'Jules Favre N⁰ 2,' from the Gare du Nord at 11.30 p.m. on 30th November, arriving Belle-Isle-en-Mer (Morbihan) at 8 a.m. on 1st December. 548 kilometres. Aeronaut: Martin. Our offensive against the Prussians has been speeded up because of information that the enemy has been sending its best troops to the Loire. As soon as General Ducrot learned this he called a meeting of the War Council, and urged immediate action. He said that further delay in our offensive would be fatal, and his arguments were so convincing that the attack is to be launched immediately.

Three proclamations were issued to the people of Paris; one by the Government of National Defence, another by General Trochu, and a third by General Ducrot. General Ducrot's manifesto was received enthusiastically because Parisians liked its fighting spirit.

['The time has come to burst the ring of steel that has encircled us for too long,' wrote General Ducrot. 'I am resolved and I swear this before you, before the whole nation: I will return to Paris dead or victorious; you may see me fall, but you will not see me retreat. If I fall, go forward and avenge me!']

The army, the Mobiles, and the National Guard are all galvanized. The battalions from Auteuil and Passy swung through the streets this morning, while their womenfolk bade them farewell. Members of the National Guard shouted: 'We don't mind being killed by the Prussians, but death to the Bonapartists!'

General Ducrot's army is marching against Versailles while General Vinoy has gone to reinforce General d'Aurelle de Paladines's army of the Loire at Orleans.

30th November 1870. The decree forbidding our newspapers from divulging military preparations has met with general approval.

The attack directed against Thiais the day before yesterday was a feint to prevent the enemy from noticing the main movement by General Ducrot's army, of which a corps under the command of General Bellemare had to cross the Marne at Charenton. The engineers threw a bridge across by night, but the Prussians blew up the dam at Neuilly-sur-Marne, and the bridge was washed away.

This was the news, grossly exaggerated by the newspapers, that caused alarm in Paris, and made the Government decree a censorship.

In fact, General Bellemare was successful three hours later in crossing the Seine, where he joined up with General Ducrot, who is now said to have pierced the enemy's lines at Saint-Denis.

Gunfire has been violent and uninterrupted from Saint-Denis to Choisy-le-Roi since two o'clock this morning. It comes from the forts at Charenton, Nogent, Saint-Maur, and Ivry, and the barrage is to protect the crossing of the Marne by our troops at Nogent.

The enemy brought up heavy reinforcements during the night.

Ambulances have been leaving Paris since dawn to bring back the wounded. There is a rumour that as soon as General Trochu took up his position on the plateau of Avron the Germans destroyed the lock gates of the Chelles Canal, flooding the country below.

6th December 1870. The military operations, at a standstill since the battle of 2nd December, will soon start again. General Trochu visited the fort at Vincennes during the day, and though he is satisfied with our recent victories a friend who saw him tells me that he is calm and prudent. He said:

'I am hopeful, but we 've still much to do.'

He added that he had no news of the provincial armies, but that he had dispatched several messengers with detailed instructions, so that all the different moves should be co-ordinated.

General Trochu, following the operations of 2nd December, was anxious to continue on the left bank of the Marne. General Ducrot decided he wanted to recross to the right bank. As the two generals could not agree they chose the acting Minister of Marine as arbitrator, who opted for General Ducrot.

The main result of the engagements of 29th and 30th November and of 2nd December has been to raise the morale of our army, and to bring out the heroism of our officers, who are worthy of those fine words of General de Charrière:

'If we have an army that knows how to die, France is saved.'

The Prussians certainly suffered heavy casualties on 2nd December, which is not surprising in view of the heavy forces they massed on the marshy ground at Chelles, dominated by the forts of Nogent and Rosny and our batteries at Avron. As soon as the Germans advanced the heavy guns from our batteries mowed them down, and they were obliged to withdraw.

General Hugues is now in command of 12,000 men on the plateau of Avron, and the Germans will doubtless try to dislodge him in spite of a battery of naval guns which makes his position extremely strong.

Paris has learned with great sorrow that our army of the Loire has been repulsed, and Orleans retaken by the Prussians. This news was brought to General Trochu by an envoy from M. de Moltke, who offered to take a member of General Trochu's staff to see for himself. The general refused.

7th December 1870. I walked down the boulevards last evening. Everywhere I heard people praising General Trochu for his answer to General de Moltke, and there was great satisfaction that the Government of National Defence has decided to continue the struggle until the bitter end. The news of the defeat of our army of the Loire has not caused a single person to give up hope. All honest folk and true patriots are loud in their praises for the energetic measures taken against Flourens's gangs at Belleville, and for the various measures to restore order whether in the National Guard or in a number of battalions of the Mobile Guard. Military discipline has been withheld far

too long from certain infamous hooligans who dishonour the French uniform. Since 31st October, though there was a warrant out for his arrest, Flourens was able to go about Paris as he pleased, and was successful in placing himself at the head of his scouts at the risk of compromising our operations against the enemy. The legal proceedings started more than a month ago against Flourens and his companions are still held up. This weakness is deplorable. Will the Government, after these fresh scandals, decide to arrest him?

General de Moltke's action in dispatching an emissary to General Trochu is considered by some members of the Government as a preliminary to a peace plan. The Prussian general appears to say:

'Your provincial army is now wiped out. You can no longer hope for any help from outside, and in this case it is impossible for you to continue the war. Lay down your arms and let us talk things over.'

As Orleans fell on 4th December it is not surprising that the Government did not receive any pigeons bringing details of that day's fighting, but why have we not received any news from Tours?

A War Council was held to-day, and our generals were rather more optimistic, having heard that General Bourbaki[1] and General Chanzy have formed two separate armies of what is left of the scattered army of the Loire. They claim that Bourbaki has already manœuvred skilfully, and has even engaged the enemy with success.

[1] In December 1798 a Greek mariner from Cephalonia made a perilous journey from Marseilles to Alexandria on behalf of General Bonaparte. His grandson, Charles Bourbaki, admitted during the reign of Louis-Philippe to the Royal Military College of La Flèche, became the Emperor Napoleon III's most brilliant young general. On a July evening in 1870, Bourbaki was descending the grand staircase of the Tuileries when the emperor passed him on the way up to his apartments. 'General,' said Napoleon III, 'it is my desire that you should take command of the Imperial Guard.'

At the age of fifty-four, Charles Bourbaki, therefore, found himself at the head of the finest command in the French army.

When the Franco-Prussian War broke out, Bourbaki led the Imperial Guard into cavalry action—a glorious chapter in this unhappy war—but in September he found himself in Metz chafing under the inaction imposed by Marshal Bazaine, the Commander-in-Chief. Bourbaki became the leader of a number of generals who wanted to organize a desperate break through the Prussian armies that surrounded the town.

Bazaine, already in intelligence with the Prussians, was afraid of this impulsive young general, and the marshal plotted with the enemy to get rid of him. On 15th September Bourbaki was returning to camp when a staff

8th December 1870. General Trochu is taking advantage of the weather, which has been holding up operations, to reorganize our army, and put it into a fit state to resume the great offensive. He is also anxiously waiting for news from General Bourbaki to co-ordinate the work of our two armies. Signals have been

---

officer handed him a note on which Marshal Bazaine had written these words in pencil:

'Her Majesty the Empress Regent having ordered the Divisional General Bourbaki, Commander of the Imperial Guard, to report to her; permission is hereby granted.' Signed: Bazaine. Metz. 15th September 1870.

Unable to understand this strange note, Bourbaki did not dismount from the horse he was riding, but went straight to headquarters, where he was received by the marshal's aide-de-camp, General Boyer.

Boyer pointed through an open window to the Commander-in-Chief, who was walking in the garden with a stranger.

'You doubtless know that gentleman?' said Boyer. 'Have you not seen him at the Tuileries? His name is Régnier.'

'He is totally unknown to me,' answered Bourbaki. 'And what can there be in common between the empress and this suspicious-looking individual?'

A few moments later Bazaine came in with Régnier.

'I imagine you will not refuse to go to Chislehurst?' he asked.

'This is the position,' Régnier broke in. 'M. de Bismarck is not anxious to treat with Jules Favre and the Government of National Defence. He would like to approach the empress, who is unwilling to commit herself before consulting you.'

Bourbaki answered that he would only go to England if the marshal gave him written instructions. These were issued, and Bourbaki left on 24th September with Régnier, who turned out to be a Prussian agent in Bismarck's pay.

The empress showed utter surprise when Bourbaki arrived. When, however, Bourbaki tried to return to Metz, the Germans refused to give him a safe-conduct. He therefore went to Tours, where he was enthusiastically received by Gambetta, who put him in charge of the north of France. He was told to raise a relief army and march on Paris.

On 20th November he was called back to take command of the 18th corps of the army of the Loire. He reached Orleans only four days before the city was captured by the Germans, and only just had time to draw back to Gien, while General Chanzy, in command of the sixteenth and seventeenth corps, drew back on Blois.

General d'Aurelle de Paladines, in disgrace, was relieved of his command by the Delegation at Tours.

[Some historians consider Régnier's relationship with the Prussians as not proven, but Commandant Grandin gives this account in his *Bourbaki.* Paris, 1898.]

arranged between the two generals so that the army of Paris may learn of the approach of Bourbaki's army. These signals will be visible at a great distance. If Bourbaki can arrive with 100,000 men, Trochu and Ducrot believe that they can at last raise the siege.

10th December 1870. By balloon 'Général Renault' from the Gare du Nord at 2.15 a.m. on 11th December, arriving Baillolet (Seine-Inférieure) at 5.30 a.m. 143 kilometres. Aeronaut: Joignerey. The latest news from Tours suggests that Gambetta has placed Republicans from southern France in the ranks of the army of the Loire, and that these elements are spreading insubordination. When Bourbaki went to Tours on 16th November it was decided that the least efficient regiments would be left at Orleans, and that those in which more confidence could be placed, numbering some 50,000 men, would be put under the command of General d'Aurelle de Paladines, and try to join up with Bourbaki.

The Government believes that General Michel was at the head of the army of Orleans, which was beaten on 4th December by the Prussians. While the enemy was marching against General Michel, therefore, General de Paladine's army was on its way to meet that of Bourbaki.

During last night two pigeons were brought to General Trochu bearing forged telegrams. One of these announced that Rouen had been occupied and that the Germans were approaching Cherbourg; the other spoke of panic in the south. Both these dispatches—in very bad French—had been written by the Prussians, and signed with the names of well-known Frenchmen, one of whom, unfortunately for the Germans, is now in Paris!

General Ducrot was asked if he had any objection to his name being given to a new balloon. The general answered:

'It's kind of you to have thought of me, but I'd rather you waited a few more days. I may then be more worthy of the honour.'

The wonderful château of the Duke of Pozzo di Borgo at Montretout has been burned to the ground by the Prussians.

14th December 1870. Had it not been for the bad weather important operations would have started to-day. General Trochu seems certain that Bourbaki is nearing Paris.

Precautions are being taken to safeguard our troops on the plateau of Avron from German surprise attacks. Our position there limits the enemy's movements in the direction of Chelles and Gagny.

M. Dupuy de Lôme, who claims to have discovered a way of steering balloons, has not yet given any public demonstration. Nevertheless, because of his official position as Director of the Balloon Service, he has been able to prevent any encouragement being given to a young inventor who makes a similar claim.

This balloon is on show at the Gare de l'Ouest. It has the shape of a fish, and when rising looks like an ungainly porpoise. The car is a streamlined wicker basket; the ventilators are of polished spruce, and are made to look like fins, and the envelope is seventeen yards long. The inventor is called Smitter. He has been working on his idea for fifteen years, and as the Government refused to advance him the necessary capital to build the ship, his friends clubbed together and lent him 6,000 francs, but now that everything is ready M. Dupuy de Lôme refuses to allow the balloon to take the air until he has publicly demonstrated his own dirigible.

M. Smitter spends all day at the Gare de l'Ouest explaining his invention to eager crowds.

PS. An agent of General Bourbaki, having managed to cross the Prussian lines, arrived in Paris this afternoon.

15th December 1870. I ended my last letter with the news that a messenger had reached us from the provinces. This man claims that General d'Aurelle de Paladines is in the department of the Orne (Lower Normandy), and that he is marching to link up with Bourbaki.

Some members of the Government are almost optimistic. Mr

Washburne, the United States minister, is less encouraging. He claims that our relief armies are in a bad way. You will remember that I told you that Mr Washburne promised M. de Bismarck that he would not show us any newspapers from outside. He is so anxious not to break his word that, having to remain in bed with a chill, he tucks his newspapers under his pillow!

If our relief armies are really in such a bad way as Mr Washburne would like us to believe, why does M. de Bismarck not let us see the newspapers? The Prussians do not often neglect their propaganda.

I think we can take it for granted that the Russian military attaché will not return to Paris. Members of the Jockey Club made no pretence of hiding their feelings about the frequent trips made by this diplomat between Paris and the Prussian headquarters. His foster-brother is an aide-de-camp to the King of Prussia, and many are tempted to think that he has been spying, not only for Russia, but also for Prussia.

The newspapers claim that Rouen has been occupied by the Germans, but that the enemy has been repulsed from Le Mans. Our troops are said to be resisting energetically in the Sarthe.

16th December 1870. By balloon 'Le Parmentier' from the Gare d'Orléans at 1.20 a.m. on 17th December, arriving Gourgançon (Marne) at 9 a.m. 150 kilometres. Aeronaut: Louis Paul. Following a day of conflicting rumours, it appears that Mr Washburne's pessimism was justified, but in spite of the reverses of our relief armies Parisians are by no means discouraged. They find it less depressing to be told bad news than none at all. Moreover, the fact that our provincial armies suffer occasional reverses proves that we are not fighting quite alone, and the fortunes of war that are against us to-day may turn in our favour to-morrow.

Our chief concern is for the Government to renew an offensive with the 250,000 stout-hearted, well-equipped troops now in the capital. If the provincial armies cannot come to the help of Paris, it is up to the army of Paris to break out and join up with the provinces.

We have enough food to last two months, and the issue of a new set of ration books will put a stop to the initial muddling which resulted in far more cards being issued than there were members of families. Unfortunately the mortality has doubled since the beginning of the siege. The consumption of food has gone down in the same proportion.

The Government's requisition of horses guarantees an adequate meat supply until 25th February. The Paris Cab Company still owns 6,000 horses, the Omnibus Company 6,700. Since the beginning of the siege the Omnibus Company is losing an average of 30,000 francs a day. Each bus takes only 40 francs for a day's run, instead of 80 francs before the siege.

Incoming pigeons yesterday carried a great number of extremely fine leaves of collodion. Each sheet, having a surface no wider than a one-franc coin, contains 300 telegrams. A pigeon can carry ten or twenty of these leaves without noticing the weight. [This was the invention of M. Dagron, who was sent by the Government to Tours on 21st November. He photographed twelve to sixteen sheets of printed matter on a tiny film which, rolled tightly, could be slipped into the hollow part of a quill, and attached to the pigeon's tail by a piece of waxed cotton. The film was enlarged as soon as it arrived, and contained the equivalent of several thousand telegrams.]

The Government seems somewhat happier to-day. It is thought that General Chanzy has succeeded in crossing the Loire to join up with Bourbaki.

20th December 1870. We are waiting for news about the engagements on the Loire and on the Seine. Meanwhile Paris is full of rumours, some of them optimistic, others pessimistic, few of them true. There are people who say that Bourbaki and Chanzy have met, and are fighting against Prince Frederick Charles, part of whose army they have hurled into the river. Others claim the exact opposite: that Chanzy's army has been broken up.

Gambetta writes to say that volunteers are being raised everywhere in the provinces, and in a month's time we shall have 700,000 men under arms. The recent reverses of our relief armies will not, therefore, prove to be the end of their resistance.

There was a large crowd in the rue de Rivoli yesterday evening—all because a pigeon was perched on the roof of the governor's office. Parisians are so avid of news that they thought that the pigeon had just arrived from Tours with a sheaf of telegrams and they showed their impatience by a good-natured demonstration. In fact, the pigeon was one of those friendly Parisian birds that never fly more than a short distance from the heart of the city. It probably spends the major part of its quiet life on the top of the Louvre.

21st December 1870. By balloon 'Lavoisier' from the Gare d'Orléans at 2 a.m. on 22nd December, arriving La Ménitré (Maine-et-Loire) at 9 a.m. 290 kilometres. Aeronaut: Sauveur Ledret. Every available ambulance was marshalled during the night. Depots were formed at Saint-Denis, Courbevoie, and on the plateau of Avron. We are doubtless attacking simultaneously from the north-east, the south-east, and the west. The whole of our troops without exception, the National Guard, the Mobile Guard, the infantry, the *gendarmes*, both foot and horse, the sailors, and the customs men, are engaged. The last battalions of the National Guard left during the night, and *gendarmes* marched behind to deal with any who tried to run away.

27th December 1870. The attack which I described to you in my last letter developed into the second battle of Le Bourget. It proved as unsuccessful as the first (30th October), and this latest failure cost us not only the life of General Blaise, a veteran of our African army, and some 20,000 casualties (less from Prussian bullets than from the intense cold, the temperature suddenly dropping to many degrees below zero), but it has shaken the confidence of Parisians in their leaders, in themselves, and in the future of the war.

General Trochu, whose popularity was already endangered after the battle of the Marne, has returned to Paris with his prestige seriously diminished. He is being violently criticized in the newspapers and in the political clubs.

A meeting of the Defence Council was held yesterday under the presidency of General Trochu, but he was less in the presidential chair than in the witness box. He was accused simultaneously of being an incompetent soldier and a political appeaser, for M. Jules Favre and M. Picard, taking it in turns to be public prosecutor, seized this opportunity to deliver themselves of all their pent-up grievances. General Trochu, faced with this lack of confidence on the part of his colleagues, remained dignified, reading a long speech he had prepared in advance.

General Ducrot also suffers his second defeat since he left Paris after making that flamboyant speech: 'I will return to Paris dead or victorious!' He will soon be the butt of the humorists.

There are rumours that the Government has been hiding the news of a defeat to our army of the Loire for forty-eight hours.

Political circles are preoccupied by an article in *The Times* reporting the terms of an agreement between Great Britain, Prussia, and Russia. Russia would obtain advantages in the Orient; the King of Prussia would become Emperor of Germany and annex Alsace and Lorraine; Great Britain would take over Egypt—all of this while France suffers the humiliation of an army of occupation.

31st December 1870. General Trochu's latest proclamation makes no deep impression on Parisians, who say that the time for words has passed. What we need to-day is action.

The general announces a new offensive. But will this action be carried out with foresight, skill, and vigour, or will our troops be obliged to retire almost as soon as they have advanced?

During a recent meeting of the Defence Council, criticism against General Trochu was so bitter that there was talk of his resignation. M. Jules Favre said that he was disposed to vote for it if his colleagues thought it necessary. General Trochu remains governor because there is nobody to take his place. Moreover, the members of the Government realize that Paris may soon have to capitulate, and they feel that General Trochu may as well assume responsibility for this uncongenial task.

The bombardment of Paris has been going on for five days. It started on 27th December, immediately after our defeat at Le Bourget, and came as a shock to everybody. The officers in charge of our forts, however, treat the bombardment lightly, saying that the enemy will never succeed in taking Paris until it makes a siege 'according to the rules.'

General Trochu is cultivating the friendship of the Republican members of his Government. He now says that the Republic is the only possible form of government for France, and his critics claim that he is anxious to become our first president.

A messenger carrying telegrams from General Chanzy, dated 19th December, has successfully crossed the enemy lines. In these dispatches General Chanzy treats the Government with a certain degree of sarcasm. He says that Bourbaki can hold up the army of Prince Frederick Charles, and that he, Chanzy, can beat the Prince of Mecklenburg and march towards Paris, but that he must know whether the Paris army is capable of breaking out and coming to his help. On receipt of this news the messenger was given 10,000 francs, and the War Council drew up plans for a new campaign.

3rd January 1871. By balloon 'Newton' from the Gare d'Orléans at 4 a.m. on 4th January, arriving Digny (Eure-et-Loir) at 11.15 a.m. 110 kilometres. Aeronaut: Aimé Ours. This is the eighth day of the bombardment. This operation, which must be very costly for the Germans, has not so far seriously damaged any of our forts or shaken the morale of our civilian population. Indeed, it may be put down as a complete failure for Germany, which will gain nothing from it but world-wide reprobation for an odious act.

Our military engineers say that the Germans would need breach batteries at not more than 100 yards to destroy our forts, and if the Germans try this they will find themselves within range of our heavy naval guns. Eighty very heavy guns have just been mounted at a place I cannot name. These guns are destined to destroy the enemy batteries at Raincy, Gagny, and the bridge of Gournay, and to force the Prussians to abandon Montfermeil.

While military operations all round Paris are being renewed with increased vigour, diplomatic negotiations are taking place, especially with England. M. Chaudordy, a delegate of our Ministry of Foreign Affairs, is in London, and if M. Thiers is not there already he will arrive shortly. M. Thiers is being criticized for having said that it may be necessary to give up Alsace to save Lorraine.

5th January 1871. The bombardment, which never ceases all through the night, redoubled in intensity at dawn. While the Prussians are concentrating their fire on the north-east, the south-east, and the south-west, our troops are taking the offensive near Bicêtre, Issy, Montrouge, and Vanves. Mont-Valérien has joined in the action.

This is the start of the operations decided on at the last War Council. The new guns recently mounted on our forts have been firing this morning for the first time, and the Prussians are now having a taste of their own medicine. In preparation for to-day's attack, the College of Vanves has been evacuated, and the wounded are being brought back from Saint-Denis. Our attack is not yet fully developed, for many battalions of the National Guard and the Mobile Guard are still being re-formed.

The Government believes that General Chanzy is approaching Paris. Parisians are so engrossed in the possible arrival of this relief army that when a man on horseback cantered down the Champs-Élysées this morning shouting out that a provincial army was at the gates of Paris, the crowds were disposed to believe him.

In order to husband our supplies of flour the Paris loaf now contains 50 per cent wheat, 30 per cent rice, and 20 per cent oats. Perhaps I should say that this is what it is supposed to contain. In fact, a great deal of bread is much less palatable than this. I shudder to think what it is made of.

6th January 1871. German prisoners captured by our troops

Light Infantry during the Siege of Paris. From a contemporary Drawing

Uhlans tracking the Course of a Balloon during the Siege of Paris

on the plateau of Avron state that since the bombardment the Crown Prince has left Versailles with 60,000 men to reinforce the army of Prince Frederick Charles. This seems hardly credible. Is this long-distance bombardment, then, nothing but a blind to cover the departure of the Crown Prince? Some of our generals seem willing to believe it. They urge General Trochu to find out if the Prussian army round Paris is smaller than it was. General Chanzy complains that we have allowed the Duke of Mecklenburg's army to slip away and attack the army of the Loire.

Parisians are enduring the bombardments calmly. They even joke about them. Ruined buildings, fire brigades clanging down the streets, ambulances bringing away a few dead and wounded provide a stirring spectacle. Shells burst during the night in the heart of the city, at the Place de l'Observatoire, in front of the statue of Marshal Ney, and in the gardens of the Luxembourg.

It is said that our army of the north-east is composed of 90,000 men, and is waiting for reinforcements numbering 30,000.

Posters were seen on many walls to-day calling on the population to revolt against the Government.

7th January 1871. The bombardment went on all night and this morning with increased violence. This is now the twelfth day and, except for some sightseeing and a lot of gossip, the population goes about its daily business as if nothing unusual were happening. Most of the destruction, so far, has taken place on the south bank of the Seine. A large number of shells fell yesterday on an ambulance post in the grounds of a home for aged people at Auteuil, from which flew the flag of Geneva. Nobody was hurt, and the hospital nurses hunted for shrapnel.

Members of No. 6 sector of the National Guard at Meudon and Saint-Cloud shelter during bombardments under the arches of the Métropolitain railway.

The appeals for a revolution by the bandits of the Commune have had no effect; but everybody blames the Government for being so weak with these miserable allies of the enemy.

9th January 1871. By balloon 'Gambetta' from the Gare du Nord at 3.30 a.m. on 10th January, arriving Avallon (Yonne) at 2.30 p.m. 200 kilometres. Aeronaut: Charles Duvivier. Parisians have been queuing up all the morning in front of the posters announcing the latest news from the provinces—the excellent situation of our relief armies and the victory of the army of the north under General Faidherbe. These telegrams are received with restraint, but with confidence. The public believes in its speedy delivery.

General Trochu, who has shown signs of discouragement of late, now seems full of hope, but he realizes, as we all do, that it is a fight against time, for our food reserves are rapidly dwindling. The Government has doubtless made this fact clear to our relief armies, urging them to hurry. Has General Faidherbe, following his great victory at Bapaume on 3rd January, been able to arrive any nearer to Paris?

10th January 1871. By balloon 'Képler' from the Gare d'Orléans at 3.30 a.m. on 11th January, arriving Montigné près Laval (Mayenne) at 9.15 a.m. 283 kilometres. Aeronaut: Roux. The more the Government releases good news about our provincial armies, the more the population of Paris becomes impatient at Trochu's inactivity. The governor's friends point out that his policy is a wise one because, if the besieging German armies have to march away to fight Faidherbe and our three army corps in the east, then Paris will find itself automatically freed.

Only yesterday the Government was impressing on us the necessity of keeping General Bourbaki's march eastwards a great secret. During the afternoon we received the Berlin newspapers dated 2nd January, and as soon as we opened them we found all the details of this ill-kept secret!

The *Journal des Débats* is exposing the people who still keep luxury horses in spite of the fact that our crack cavalry regiments are obliged to kill their mounts to provide food. This newspaper is unfortunately quite right. I know a wealthy official of the Ministry of Finance who has eight horses, and the fine ladies who have stayed in Paris have nearly all kept theirs. A pretty society woman, who does canteen work, has a mare worth 7,000 francs. This public exposure will probably tighten the regulations.

The latest rumour is that Bourbaki's march eastwards is towards Berlin, where he will free our prisoners!

11th January 1871. The bombardment of the forts, which began on 27th December, has now reached its sixteenth day, and the bombardment of the centre of Paris, which started on 5th January, has now reached its seventh day. None of the forts has fallen, and the shelling of the civilian population, which has caused the deaths of elderly people, women, and babies, has produced a wave of fury amongst the population and a cry for vengeance.

Last night's bombardment was particularly sharp on Grenelle, Vaugirard, a section of the Faubourg Saint-Germain, the Latin Quarter, and the residential districts of Passy and Auteuil. From ten o'clock last night till four o'clock this morning a rain of shells fell on Auteuil from the heights of Saint-Cloud. The population was too frightened to sleep, and women, clutching their babies, rushed out of the falling houses. It was a picture of desolation and anger, especially on the part of the women, who shouted to their husbands and brothers:

'You're a lot of cowards to allow this to go on without fighting back. Why don't you go and attack the Prussian batteries?'

This feeling dominates Paris, and will oblige General Trochu to abandon his policy of inaction. Last night's violent bombardment did a great deal of damage to property, but there were few fatal casualties.

General Trochu has written to Moltke asking if it is pure coincidence that nearly all our big hospitals have been systematically shelled—the Hospital for Sick Children, the Salpétrière, the Val-de-Grâce, the Hôpital de la Pitié, and others. It seems almost certain that the Prussians are doing this on purpose as a form of terror warfare.

14th January 1871. By balloon 'Vaucanson' from the Gare d'Orléans at 3 a.m. on 15th January, arriving Erquinghem (Nord) at 11 a.m. 240 kilometres. Aeronaut: André Clariot. The bombardment, less strong for a couple of days, started again during the night with a violence not hitherto attained. The insides of our eastern and southern forts have been seriously damaged, but the guns can still be used. In the forts of Issy and Vanves seven guns out of eighty have been destroyed, but new ones have already been brought up to replace them.

The Prussians are beginning to realize that the bombardment of the civilian population is having no other result but to stiffen our resistance. Unfortunately, if Paris falls it will be through hunger. Our food reserves are almost exhausted.

New decrees have just been passed ordering house-to-house searches for hoarded food, especially flour. There were long queues outside the bakers' shops at 5 a.m. to-day, but shortly after they opened there was no more bread, and they were closed again till to-morrow. The bread shortage might cause a panic, and in this case the Government will no longer be able to maintain order.

Many generals have been placed on the retired list for spreading defeatist rumours.

[The battle of Buzenval (19th January), final battle of the siege, took place between this letter and the next. The aim of the attack was to surprise and capture the Prussian headquarters at Versailles. The attackers numbered 100,000 men—60,000 National Guard, Mobiles, etc., and 40,000 civilians, who improvised themselves soldiers for a single day and a single battle!

Although this scratch army was badly co-ordinated, it met with initial success, but later in the day the Prussian artillery broke the attack.

By nightfall the army was routed, and famine had entered the city.

General Trochu, on his return to Paris, was relieved of his military command, but appointed his own successor, General Vinoy. At the height of this crisis (21st–22nd January) the

Anarchists committed two acts of violence—the kidnapping from jail of their leader Flourens and an attack on the Hôtel de Ville.

While Paris was being bombarded more violently than ever, Jules Favre was sent to Versailles to negotiate an armistice. It was signed, on 28th January, at the very moment that historic Saint-Cloud was in flames.

Of this armistice General Trochu wrote later:

'I was stupefied by the harshness and the inhumanity with which the Germans applied the conditions of this armistice on the conquered.'

Elections for the new Assembly were fixed for 8th February.]

VII. THE ARMISTICE

1ST *February 1871.* Public opinion in Paris, at first undecided about what powers should be conferred on the coming National Assembly, is now of the opinion that this body should have sovereign rights. In fact, the question will have to be decided by the Assembly itself.

2nd February 1871. The Duc de la Tremoïlle has just arrived from Bordeaux, which he left on 20th January. He was obliged to make a long detour, travelling by way of Basle and Strasburg, and brings us surprising news. He claims that M. Thiers, much discouraged, plays a relatively minor role. Gambetta is the dominating figure. He is in complete command, and is obeyed by everybody. Fresh provincial troops were being raised in great numbers, but they were badly equipped and officered and ill fed. The Breton battalions refused to fight because their rifles were out of date, although they engaged the enemy once to show that they were not frightened of exposing their lives.

During his journey across France the duke found many departments ravaged. He saw ruination and despair everywhere.

Though there is considerable trade between Alsace and Lorraine and Germany, these two provinces remain faithful to France, and all the women in Strasburg wear mourning to show their protestation and defiance of the foreign tyrant.

The duke travelled from Versailles with M. Jules Favre.

M. Ducroux, who was Prefect of Police in 1848, is now managing director of the Paris Cab Company. He has left by balloon to buy horses in the provinces, for the company has only 1,500 left—6,000 were eaten by the population during the siege.

The Baron Alphonse de Rothschild has refused to be nominated by Paris and the Seine-et-Marne for the National Assembly, believing that he can render more important services to his country during the coming days of reconstruction by remaining at the head of the great banking house. He feels that if he were elected a member of the Assembly he would no longer be at liberty to take part in any financial operation.

3rd February 1871. What a terrible balance sheet the National Assembly will be called upon to draw up! Civil engineering firms are planning huge public works programmes to employ men demobilized from the army and the Mobile Guards.

A big convoy of food on its way to Paris was pillaged during the night. The National Guard has been called on to protect future convoys.

4th February 1871. Parisians read with interest posters announcing that the Duc d'Aumale [fourth son of Louis-Philippe and uncle of the Comte de Paris] has put forward his name as a candidate in the department of the Seine for the National Assembly.

His action has given rise to comment. Some people declare that the duke's candidature for the modest role of deputy is simply the first step towards becoming president of the Assembly, and finally head of the State. This manœuvre, successful with Louis-Napoleon, is not likely to work twice.

This does not mean that people are hostile to a monarchy. Far from it. But they would prefer a clear choice between a restoration of the Bourbon dynasty in the person of the Comte de Chambord, united with his Orleanist cousins, and a Republic.

Meanwhile the Government of National Defence is in rapid disintegration. All its members will resign as soon as the National Assembly is formed and a chief of executive power will be elected to govern until such time as the Assembly decides what form the future constitution of France will take.

The National Assembly is unlikely to choose Bordeaux as its seat of government. Gambetta, backed by the Demagogic party in central and southern France, will probably make a determined bid to dominate the new Parliament. His party is strong in Bordeaux, and he has drafted into this city several Red battalions of the National Guard from Lyons. As no regular troops may be moved from their present positions during the armistice, and as only one brigade is stationed in Bordeaux, I think the National Assembly may feel even less secure there than in Paris.

General Trochu says that in spite of being so violently attacked from every side he receives countless requests every day for decorations and medals from those very people who, in public, are most unkind to him. The Government, it is true, has abolished the Cross of the Legion of Honour for civilians, but as every civilian is, or has been, in the National Guard, the abolition of this decoration is a myth.

M. Henri Rochefort, the famous journalist who, in the *Lanterne*, so violently attacked Napoleon III during the Second Empire, is championing M. Gambetta. In his new paper, *Le Mot d'Ordre*, he publishes a manifesto by Gambetta, in which the fiery young Republican says:

'I will have nothing to do with the armistice. It was signed with culpable negligence, against my advice.'

Here is a pretty state of affairs! The National Assembly will require much wisdom and energy to ·guide us through such troubled waters.

7th February 1871. The refusal of Gambetta to recognize the armistice is passed over in silence by the *Journal Officiel*. M. Jules Simon and his colleagues of the Paris Government were received in Bordeaux by boos and catcalls, and were obliged to leave town immediately. The *Journal Officiel* is equally silent about this grave incident. Nevertheless, we are entitled to know whether we have one Government or two.

The *Mot d'Ordre* says:

'There is grave unrest in the south of France. Many delegations have arrived from Marseilles, Lyons, and Toulouse, entreating Gambetta to make himself dictator, to charge the Paris Government with treason, and to continue the war to the bitter end. We are not down and out. The National Guards are still mobilized, and are full of enthusiasm, eager to march against the enemy.'

Bismarck, admirably informed about what is going on at Bordeaux and in the south of France, has told M. Jules Favre that if the Paris Government is unable to make itself respected, the armistice will be cancelled and the Prussians will restore order in France.

PS. I have just heard from Bordeaux that M. Gambetta has resigned.

9th February 1871. In truth we have no more Government. The National Assembly must lose no time before electing a chief of executive power. When this new body has chosen delegates for the painful mission of negotiating a peace treaty it will, I am told, appoint a committee to inquire into the causes of our defeat, so that justice can be meted out to those who are responsible. Some candidates are promising to bring Napoleon III, his ministers, and a number of marshals and generals to trial.

The first ballots for the National Assembly yesterday favour Louis Blanc, Gambetta, Garibaldi, Victor Hugo, and Edgar Quinet. M. Thiers will probably be elected. The early returns, which appear to favour the Socialists, can easily prove misleading.

General Le Flô, the Minister for War, has been asked by Bismarck to organize an army of 10,000 men at Bordeaux to protect the National Assembly. General d'Aurelle de Paladines may be placed in command.

11th February 1871. The election results are coming in very slowly because the Prussians have limited us to a single telegraph wire between Paris and Versailles.

Even if M. Jules Favre is not elected, he will help M. Thiers to negotiate the peace treaty. Bismarck insists on this because he has been treating with our Foreign Minister ever since the first conference at Ferrières.

Epidemics of typhus are reported in several outlying districts of Paris, occupied by the Germans.

13th February 1871. Nominations in fifty departments for the National Assembly are announced to-day, M. Thiers has been elected thirteen times, and will receive at least fifteen nominations. His name stands for peace, order, and constitutional monarchy.

The new Assembly will be similar to that of 1848, with a Conservative majority composed of Legitimists, Orleanists, and moderate Republicans.

Prince Napoleon [brother of Princess Mathilde] has been elected in Corsica; but will he dare return to Paris?

M. Thiers, M. Jules Favre, and the Comte Alexandre Chaudordy are likely to be chosen as the three delegates to discuss peace terms. General d'Aurelle de Paladines and General Faidherbe will probably accompany them to the Prussian headquarters.

15th February 1871. As my latest mail from Bordeaux is dated 12th February you will see that the postal services are not yet back to normal. My correspondents tell me that large meetings are being held by our future deputies, and that M. Thiers's influence is greater than anybody's.

The National Assembly is to sit at Versailles, where the Government will also have its headquarters. Some members objected that Versailles, being so near to Paris, might be invaded by revolutionary bands, which, since 1789, have not failed to break up such bodies. Others pointed out that if danger threatened the Assembly an urgent telegram could always be sent to warn the authorities in time.

17th February 1871. My politician friends in Bordeaux say that the majority of the Assembly would prefer to call on the country to continue the war rather than accept humiliating peace terms. They feel that our war effort might be more successful if it were backed by a properly elected Government.

We see a good many German officers since the armistice. All of them say that they are tired of the war and want to go home.

It is unlikely that the Prussians will hold a victory march through the streets of Paris. The Emperor William would have to ride at the head of it, and he would run a serious risk of assassination from some of our Red leaders, who hold very definite views about the armistice.

It is lucky for some deputies that, owing to the general upheaval, no questions were asked about their qualifications. There is a deputy for Paris called Georges Clemenceau who was mayor of the XVIIIth ward.

18th February 1871. The appointment of M. Thiers as Chief of Executive Power is likely to facilitate the peace talks, give France more credit abroad, and hasten a return of confidence at home. M. Thiers will be called upon to deal with political passions, however, more violent and more anarchical than in 1848. Already the ultra-Radical press is foaming.

M. Grévy, the president of the National Assembly, is a good, honest Republican, who has always taken care to tread a middle path. He is distant, self-controlled, though perhaps not sufficiently firm to deal with the opposition that he is bound to meet from the Socialists and Communists.

20th February 1871. From letters I have received from Bordeaux I learn that there were some lively scenes when the various parties composing the majority met during the night of 16th–17th February to discuss the motion appointing M. Thiers Chief of the Executive Power of the French Republic.

The Conservatives, who numbered 250, unanimously decided to strike out the words 'French Republic.' A similar resolution was adopted by 160 Legitimists.

These 410 members wanted to make it clear that they only considered the Republic of 4th September a stepping-stone to a restoration of the monarchy.

M. Thiers, theoretically an Orleanist, insisted, however, that his title should be 'Chief of the Executive Power *of the French Republic.*' In this he was strongly supported by M. Grévy.

The question was referred back to the various political parties, who ended by accepting M. Thiers's amendment, safeguarding themselves by the phrase 'until such time as they [the words "French Republic"] are placed on the Statute Book.'

This left the door ajar.

M. Thiers and M. Jules Favre are going to Versailles to-morrow to begin peace negotiations.

Here are the members of the Cabinet announced by M. Thiers:

Interior	Ernest Picard
Foreign Affairs	Jules Favre
War	Le Flô
Marine	Pothuau
Justice	Dufaure
Public Works	Baron de Larcy
Commerce	Lambrecht

The Finances are reserved for M. Buffet, whose election has not yet been confirmed.

28th February 1871. As a result of Anarchist agitation against the peace treaty, the German regiments which had started to leave our territory have received counter-orders. Several Prussian army corps have taken up positions near our forts. If the Anarchists continue making trouble, the Germans will draft 200,000 troops into Paris on 2nd March, and keep them there for a couple of months, instead of 30,000, which is the number they announce for their two days' occupation of the capital.

M. Thiers, M. Jules Favre, and M. Picard have warned the country that if the armistice is broken the whole of France will be ravaged and new catastrophes will descend upon us. Unfortunately our troops have been left idle since the armistice, and lack of discipline has made many thousands of them easy prey for Red agitators. Infantrymen, Mobile Guards, and even sailors, who were always famous for discipline, took part in the mass meetings at the Bastille.

M. Thiers, on his return to Bordeaux from Versailles, took up residence at the Hôtel de la Préfecture. The last informal reception was held the night before he moved in—men in frock coats and women in black. The Duchess Decazes, whose husband is a member of the National Assembly, alone wore ceremonial dress.

In Paris Mme Thiers used to fall asleep every evening, while her guests were talking after dinner. Now that she is the first lady of the land, it will be interesting to see if she succeeds in keeping awake.

2nd March 1871. This is the second day of the Prussian occupation of Paris.

The night passed quietly. The enemy is billeted with the inhabitants of the VIIIth, XVIth, and XVIIth wards. French sentries are posted round the occupied sections of the city, and the Prussians are not supposed to go beyond the limits of these sections, so that they are almost prisoners in the reserved areas.

No Prussian has dared interfere with the black crape shrouding the heads of the statues of the lost provinces of Alsace and Lorraine in the Place de la Concorde.

The entrance of the Élysée on the Faubourg Saint-Honoré is closed, but that on the garden side facing the Champs-Élysées is open. Prussian inspectors are stationed in the telegraph offices of the Champs-Élysées, the Ternes, and the avenue de la Grande Armée. These are in the occupied zones. All the shops are closed, and most private houses fly a black flag, while the majority of the population remains indoors in spite of the splendour of the spring weather.

There was a slight disturbance this morning when Prussian soldiers, pipe in mouth, crossed the gardens of the Tuileries, the Carrousel, the courtyard of the Louvre, and began to wander along the quays. They were unarmed, but the public did not hide its indignation, having been promised by the Prussian High Command that no German soldier would go beyond the Place de la Concorde. I came across one of our staff officers in the courtyard of the Palais-Royal, and told him that in my opinion if General Vinoy allowed enemy troops to visit our museums and saunter through the Louvre there would be serious clashes before nightfall. He went to make a report to General Vinoy.

Many individuals suspected of being German officers in civilian clothes have been arrested by our police.

The Germans will leave Paris to-morrow morning.

3rd March 1871. On my way home at seven o'clock last evening, the Champs-Élysées were practically deserted. It was a warm starlit night, with a full moon. From time to time a few German soldiers marched rowdily past singing their native songs.

I was awakened at 4 a.m. by bugles announcing the departure of the enemy. The troops formed up in the Champs-Élysées, and, after being reviewed, marched off at seven o'clock, with bands playing.

By 10.30 the Champs-Élysées were completely evacuated without incident, except that a shot was fired by somebody at the disappearing column.

Paris has now become normal again. The Mobile Guards will leave for the provinces at the end of the week.

M. Thiers is drawing up a plan of campaign against the Paris Demagogues, who have assumed a most threatening attitude. A division of the regular army is to be brought from Bordeaux, and the *chasseurs* and the *gendarmes* are to be strengthened.

Though M. Thiers was anxious for the National Assembly to meet in Paris, the deputies, frightened by the Communist peril, will not hear of it. They want to meet at Versailles or at Fontainebleau.

6th March 1871. Admiral Pothuau, who has just reached Paris to take up his duties at the Ministry of Marine, told friends this morning that M. Thiers is worried by Demagogic propaganda in the National Guard. Anarchists have turned Montmartre and Belleville into an armed camp.

M. Thiers is determined to put a stop to this state of affairs, which is paralysing business and is doing us incalculable harm on the Continent, as well as preventing security and work at home. 'Unless order is restored,' he says, 'we cannot reorganize our army or our civil service, overhaul our fiscal system, or draw up a budget.'

He thinks that as Admiral Pothuau is popular in Paris he might help Jules Favre and Ernest Picard to clean up the National Guard. The battalion commanders will be asked to attend a meeting at which they will be told that their conduct is doing the country as much harm as the Prussians. The worst battalions will be asked to return the machine-guns, rifles, and cartridges which they stole. If they refuse the Government will use force.

Fifty loyal battalions of the National Guard in the provinces have told General d'Aurelle de Paladines that they are willing to come to Paris to help keep order.

M. Thiers has sent for an architect from Bordeaux to make the necessary alterations at Versailles to house the National Assembly.

We can therefore take it for granted that Versailles has been definitely chosen for the seat of government.

8th March 1871. Paris is a little quieter, and conversations on the boulevards and in adjoining streets are less heated. Interest is centred on business difficulties, on the rising cost of rents, and the return of prisoners of war. Even the people of Montmartre and Belleville are tired of the squabbles of the National Guard, and a Belleville battalion was pursued by its womenfolk yesterday, who shouted:

'Why didn't you use your guns against the Prussians instead of running away at Le Bourget?'

If trouble breaks out again General d'Aurelle de Paladines and General Vinoy will let the Anarchists do as they please in Belleville, Montmartre, and Menilmontant, chief lairs of the Red gangs; but if they come into the centre of Paris, the army will be called out.

Several regiments of the army of the Loire have just arrived.[1] The troops say they are sick of Gambetta and of the Republic, and that the politicians at Tours did nothing but interfere with their military campaigns during the siege of Paris.

Members of the Cabinet who came back from Bordeaux last night say that a parliamentary committee is examining the financial scandals of the Tours delegation. This delegation, you will remember, was composed of members of the Defence Government sent to Tours by General Trochu, both before and during the siege, to organize resistance in the provinces. Big defence loans were issued, and the bonds shared out amongst M. Gambetta's friends.

The newspapers announced yesterday that the hall of the States-General at Versailles had been chosen for the meetings of the National Assembly. People forget that this fine hall was pulled down by Napoleon III five years ago! The National Assembly will meet in the theatre of the château.

[1] The army of the Loire was disbanded on 7th March. General Le Flô, Minister for War, in relieving General Chanzy of his command, praised him for his brilliant services. The retreat from Orleans won the admiration of the Germans, and has been studied in military academies ever since. On 11th February, General Chanzy, while on active service, learned that he had been elected to the National Assembly by his native department of the Ardennes. Placing General de Colomb in temporary charge of all the armies of the west he went to Bordeaux, taking advantage of the armistice to give a much needed rest to his troops. He used all his influence to urge a continuation of the war, saying that a dishonourable peace would inevitably have to be avenged by a future generation. He voted against the peace treaty, refusing to believe that France was unable to continue fighting. Indeed he was convinced, and he kept this conviction to the end of his life, that France could have driven the Germans from her soil. Chanzy's opinion is worthy of great respect. He fought the enemy continually during the final three months, and nobody was better acquainted with his country's war weariness. When the army of the Loire reached Laval from Le Mans, for instance, the municipal council hurried to entreat General Chanzy not to blow up the bridges! The civic dignitaries implored him not to defend their town. Chanzy was obliged to remind them of their duty. Less than a month after his army was disbanded, it was called upon to serve France again, this time during the campaign between Thiers's Government at Versailles and the Communards in Paris.

[See *Le Général Chanzy*, par Arthur Chuquet, pp. 163–75. Paris, Librairie Plon. Ouvrage couronné par l'Académie Française.]

9th March 1871. M. Fresneau, member for the Morbihan, voices the general feeling of the National Assembly when he says that Paris should be the seat of Government, but that it is necessary first of all to restore order in the capital by disarming the subversive battalions of the National Guard, and by declaring martial law. He points out that if Versailles is to be the temporary home of the Assembly, it might as well remain at Bordeaux. The truth is that the deputies are eager to be near the Bourse, the clubs, the theatres, and pretty women. These four attractions prove irresistible.

M. Joly, the architect, spent yesterday at the palace of the Élysée, from which we may conclude that M. Thiers is thinking of taking up residence there.

The heads of business houses in Paris say that a wave of prosperity followed the signing of peace, and that big orders flowed in from the provinces and from abroad. Unfortunately all this stopped with the riots of the Bastille and the insurrection in the National Guard.

The Demagogues refuse to take down the red flag in the Place de la Bastille, claiming that it is the emblem of the Radicals, the Socialists, and the Anarchists, who form the majority in Paris. Several Cabinet ministers want to have the red flag taken down. They are holding a meeting to-day to discuss whether they dare take stringent action.

13th March 1871. The Anarchist newspapers have been suppressed.

This is the first step taken by M. Thiers to re-establish order in Paris.

The National Assembly is to be protected at Versailles by a strong garrison of picked troops. If the National Guards decide to march out of Paris to attack the Assembly, the fort of Mont-Valérien and the Montretout redoubt would be sufficient to keep them back.

The hotels, lodging houses, and shops at Bordeaux are keenly disappointed that the National Assembly is to leave the town.

They have been reaping a rich harvest and charging exorbitant prices.

15th March 1871. Many deputies reproach M. Thiers for his failure to deal with the Revolutionary Committee of the National Guard. This self-appointed committee has substituted itself for staff headquarters. It calls parades, gives orders, and for the last month has been organizing a detailed plan of revolt. General Crémer, a Demagogue and a member of the Garibaldi Red-shirts, has arrived in Paris to organize the Anarchist movement.

These are questions that M. Thiers is being asked by his critics:

'Why haven't you appointed a Prefect of Police?'

'Why haven't you arrested Flourens, Blanqui, and the other Anarchist leaders, already convicted in the courts?'

'What exactly is preventing you from dissolving the Revolutionary Committee of the National Guard?'

'Can't you see that we are moving towards complete anarchy?'

M. Thiers has promised that he will propose suitable legislation at the next sitting of the National Assembly. He says he will not take up residence at the Élysée, but will live at Versailles to watch continually over the sovereign Assembly. The president of the Assembly will take up residence in the château of Louis XIV.

VIII. THE COMMUNE

18TH *March 1871.* A dreadful day has followed a sorry night. Paris is in the throes of a revolution.

At two o'clock this morning General Vinoy, acting on orders from Versailles, occupied the Place de la Bastille with an infantry regiment, a detachment of Republican Guards, and a regiment of artillery with two field guns. The red flag was hauled down from the top of the monument in the square, and troops occupied the adjacent streets.

A very small crowd, by no means hostile, approached the Place de la Bastille, more out of curiosity than anything else. Mounted police led their horses gently through the crowds to disperse them, but a moment later they gathered again. There was not a hostile cry. The gates of the Tuileries, of the court-yard of the Carrousel, and of the Louvre were closed, and neither carriages nor pedestrians allowed.

So far, so good.

The trouble started in Montmartre.

Members of the National Guard started to crack jokes with the regular troops on duty in the streets and squares.

'Those guns and rifles you've got are ours just as much as yours!' said the National Guard. 'We all fought together, didn't we? Why don't you come and have a drink?'

A short time afterwards the regular troops, and even a squadron of the Republican Guard, came down into Paris, the butts of their rifles over their shoulders, laughing and joking with the National Guard. A captain who gave an order to his men was shot dead. The guns were left unattended on the Butte-Montmartre. Several battalions of National Guards on their way from the centre of Paris to Montmartre met their fellows coming down and called out to them:

'Down with Vinoy!
'Down with Paladines!
'Long live the Republic!
'Long live Garibaldi!'

There is no longer any Government in Paris. The National Guard is master of the capital. Perhaps it is a good thing that the National Assembly decided to meet at Versailles, for that august body would certainly have been attacked by the National Guard without being defended by the regular troops.

One general and several officers of the Republican Guard are prisoners at Montmartre.

Several battalions of the National Guard, passing M. Thiers's house in the Place Saint-Georges, cried out:

'Death to Thiers!'

I need hardly add that the red flag has been hoisted again in the Place de la Bastille:[1]

---

[1] It was not until the afternoon that the rebels committed their most foul murders.

After midday General Clément Thomas, who a short time before had resigned his post as Commander-in-Chief of the National Guard, to which he was appointed by General Trochu during the siege, walked up to Montmartre in civilian clothes.

This tall, vigorous man, in his sixtieth year, was doubtless on his way to see for himself what was happening in Montmartre. He stopped to speak to a number of workmen, whom he overheard saying that General Lecomte, separated from his troops, had been arrested by the Revolutionaries and dragged away to an unknown destination.

'And who are you?' asked one of the workmen, impressed by General Clément Thomas's strong bearded face and keen eyes.

'I'm Clément Thomas. The role I played in 1848 entitles me to your respect.'

This qualification had the opposite effect to that which the general expected.

'Then you can pay your debt,' somebody shouted.

He was seized and taken to the garden of a small villa in the rue des Rosiers, in Montmartre, where General Lecomte was being insulted by about a hundred ruffians.

Both generals were later put against a wall and shot. General Lecomte's two aides-de-camp were about to be assassinated in a like manner when a youth of eighteen suddenly turned on the tyrants and shouted:

'You cowards! What have these men done to you?'

20th March 1871. The proclamations issued by the new Government of Paris are full of honeyed words. We are told to fear no acts of violence, but already the Demagogues are fighting against each other. It is the Socialist party of the Internationale that has seized power. The more exalted revolutionaries like Louis Blanc, Blanqui, and Flourens are furious at being excluded. We must expect bitter struggles between the two camps.

Victor Hugo favours the new Government, but 30,000 criminals and convicts expelled by General Trochu after 4th September 1870 have rallied to its flag. It is also backed by the Red elements of the army, especially the infantry, who are determined to shed blood.

The whole of M. Thiers's Cabinet is now at Versailles, where the National Assembly will sit. General Vinoy is there in command of 40,000 men.

The Central Committee of the Republican Federation, as the new Paris Government calls itself, is already short of money. Thiers's Minister of Finance, before leaving Paris, took all the available funds, and the chief banks, such as the Bank of France, the Comptoir d'Escompte, and the Crédit Foncier, have long ago hidden their assets in the provinces. The revolutionaries must, however, pay the National Guard, and keep the public utility services going. How will they raise the money? Probably by some form of capital levy. The skeleton staff left by the Telegraph Company in Paris has been jailed—fortunately most of the employees were able to escape in time.

Some battalions of the National Guard, whose members are moderate, are now ashamed of having contributed by their slackness to the present state of affairs.

The Paris deputies and mayors are urging M. Thiers and the National Assembly to grant two concessions which, they claim, would end the revolt. These are:

1. To allow the National Guard to elect its own officers and its Commander-in-Chief.

2. To allow the people of Paris to elect forthwith a municipal council to govern the capital.

The mayors argue that considering that M. Thiers and all his ministers abandoned Paris on Sunday, 19th March, and that since 4th September 1870 Paris has not been allowed, like all other cities, to elect a municipal council, it is not unreasonable for elections to be held.

Two Paris deputies left for Versailles last evening to put forward these requests.

24th March 1871. Most Parisians, anxious to see the end of the civil war, were delighted this morning to read the proclamation issued by Admiral Saisset announcing the concessions of the National Assembly. Admiral Saisset has been appointed Supreme Commander of the National Guard by the Paris mayors. This is his statement:

'DEAR FELLOW CITIZENS,

'I hasten to announce to you that, together with the deputies of the Seine and the mayors of Paris, we have obtained from the Government of the National Assembly:

'1. The complete recognition of your municipal franchises.

'2. The right of electing all the officers of the National Guard, as well as the General-in-Chief.'

Will these concessions satisfy the rebels?

This depends on whether the Central Committee is anxious to redress its grievances, or whether it is determined to make a complete social revolution. Whatever happens, Paris must count on itself alone. The provinces, exhausted by the war, and sickened by the intrigues of party politics, are no more willing to raise an army to restore order in Paris than they were to continue the war against Germany.

There is complete panic here.

Everybody who could has left. One sees nothing but removal vans, and the price of food is rising every day. It is like the early days of the siege.

Admiral Saisset has taken up his headquarters at the Gare Saint-Lazare to keep in close communication with Versailles. He is much influenced by two of his aides-de-camp, Major Schœlcher and Major Langlois, who continually urge him to come to terms with the rebels.

25th March 1871. Admiral Saisset misled us. The Versailles Government denies that it is willing to grant any concessions to the Paris Central Committee.

Is it that the Paris mayors and deputies are unwilling to accept a solution, or is it that the National Assembly is backing out of its offer?

If the fault is with the Central Committee it looks as if nothing short of blood and thunder will satisfy it, but the Central Committee throws the blame on Admiral Saisset, who first announced that Versailles was willing to make concessions.

The admiral was told by the insurgents that he had better leave Paris because they could no longer guarantee his safety. He did not wait to be told twice, but threw up his command of the National Guard and left for Versailles by the next train.

Some National Guards who sympathized with the rebels at the beginning are appalled by the thought of what lies ahead. Few are brave enough to voice their feelings because they are frightened of what revenge their comrades might take. The situation is complicated by the fact that the Government is paying these men four francs a day. Many of them ask:

'Where else could we earn so much? We cannot afford to go back to work.'

The most dangerous element in the National Guard are the sharpshooters.

People who live near the barracks at Château d'Eau say they are kept awake at night by the sound of shots partly muffled by the beating of drums. Are these executions?

There have been violent scenes all day at Belleville, Batignoles, and Montmartre.

I hear from Versailles that the Cabinet is divided. Several ministers accuse their colleagues of weakness. Others say that M. Thiers is making things impossible by his irritable and dominant nature. General Le Flô, Minister of War, is considered incapable, but that is exactly why M. Thiers insists on keeping him. Our chief executive wishes to run all military matters himself.

Part of the Cabinet is calling for energetic action against the Paris rebels; M. Thiers is against this. He says that it is not possible to distinguish between the loyal and the disloyal battalions of the National Guard, and he adds: 'I do not want to have my finger caught amongst the cog-wheels for fear that my whole body may be drawn in.'

27th March 1871. After seven months of semi-starvation and distress Parisians have so great a desire for peace, for a chance to earn a living and go about their normal business, that they clutch at any hope of avoiding a civil war.

As soon as it was clear that the National Assembly was not willing to give the concessions asked for by the deputies of the Seine and by the mayors of Paris for municipal elections, the deputies and mayors decided to hold these elections immediately.

Voting started yesterday.

Parisians seem entirely satisfied and, the weather being delightful, there is a general feeling that an era of tranquillity and prosperity lies ahead.

The awakening will be rude. Antagonism remains bitter between the Socialist dictatorship in Paris and the Government at Versailles.

The municipal council (known as the Commune) will waste no time before beginning to thieve and rape; it is already divided against itself; its rifts will widen; it has no money; the Central Committee will take the cash of every public company and of all the banks, but this money will prove insufficient and the National Guard will loot and plunder. This will take place before the end of the week unless M. Thiers and the National Assembly do something.

M. Thiers's inaction is losing him ground each day. He is walking in Trochu's footsteps. He speaks well, has no initiative and no energy, counts on provincial help, and says glibly, as Trochu said, that he has a plan—a plan that will end in inertia and capitulation.

The Central Committee's representative at the Ministry of the Interior, Grélier, was so afraid of the National Guards supposed to watch over his personal safety, that he asked the ushers to show him out of the ministry by the back door, which they did. He has not been seen since.

M. de l'Espée, the new prefect of Saint-Étienne, was assassinated by the Socialists two days after he had arrived in that town to take office.

On the door of the police station of the Ternes in Paris may be seen this notice:

'The office is open from 9 a.m. to 11 a.m. and from 3 p.m. to 5 p.m. In case of absence apply to the wine shop next door.'

28th March 1871. A cry of horror and reprobation has gone up from all honest people against the abominable article in the *Journal Officiel* of Paris calling for the assassination of the Duc d'Aumale and of any prince who returns to French soil.

That a private individual, like Henri Rochefort, should glorify regicide, is an intellectual and moral depravation which concerns him alone; but for an official organ to preach murder is a monstrosity which throws a sinister light on the depths of the abyss in which we are floundering. The assassinations of Generals Lecomte and Clément Thomas and of the unfortunates at the Place Vendôme prove that men who glorify murder are assured, as in 1793, of finding people to carry out their orders. This is what is known as progress and civilization! One need only watch a march past of the battalions of insurgent National Guards to understand the situation of a capital delivered up to cut-throats!

The red flag flies from all our public buildings.

At Versailles M. Thiers continues to keep his 'plan' secret, but like Trochu he is careful to humour every political party. When the National Assembly stood in silence to pay tribute to the memory of M. de l'Espée, murdered at Saint-Étienne, four deputies of the Left remained ostentatiously seated. The parliamentary majority asked the Speaker to take disciplinary action, but in order to avoid a scandal this was refused.

The Paris mayors are asking that the National Assembly should be dissolved; they threaten to march against Versailles with 100,000 National Guards.

M. de Bismarck has written to M. Thiers to offer German help to restore order. Unless the Government masters the situation the Prussians will occupy Paris.

IX. THE COMMUNE FROM VERSAILLES

4TH *April 1871.* In danger of being trapped, arrested, and even shot if I remained any longer in Paris, I decided on Friday to hurry to Versailles, which I reached to-day after travelling by way of Saint-Germain along roads packed with refugees.

All the hotels at Saint-Germain and Versailles are full. I was lucky to obtain a lodging with friends. I am now in close touch with the Cabinet and the National Assembly, and I hope to send you all the political news. The postal services here are not so regular as in Paris, so do not blame me if my dispatches are occasionally delayed.

The telegrams dated 2nd and 3rd April, which M. Pierre sent you, gave details of the expedition begun against the insurgents, who advanced towards the bridge of Neuilly and the village of Puteaux. Our successes on both these days against the Communards are less important than the assurance we gained that our infantry can be relied on. Our troops are keen, and since last night's engagement show a real desire to get to grips with the brigands in possession of Paris.

As soon as I reached Versailles I was impressed by the smartness of the troops. They have none of the slackness in dress, the dirtiness, and the lack of discipline which make such a lamentable sight in Paris.

The deputies are right in praising M. Thiers for the way he brought the remainder of our regular army from Paris during the night of 25th March.

Our offensive against Paris started early this morning with a strong attack against the redoubt at Châtillon, which may well have fallen by now.

5th April 1871. This is the fourth day of the Government's war against the Paris Commune, and the battle is far from over.

At 3 o'clock this morning the rebels, who occupy the forts of Issy and Vanves, started to bombard our troops, who have retaken Châtillon. Our guns answered energetically, and most of the enemy fire was silenced.

Several battalions of National Guards, who left Paris during the night, crossing the woods of Meudon and Ferrières, reached the outskirts of Versailles at dawn. Our troops attacked them and threw them back.

The Commune is trying to raise an army of 100,000 men to march against Versailles. What can we do to meet the danger? So far we have about 60,000 men, of whom some were more or less seriously wounded during the war against Prussia, whilst others must be kept at Versailles to guard the ministries and the seat of Government. Our available fighting force therefore numbers some 40,000.

A call to members of the National Guard in the provinces has not proved encouraging. The provinces are tired, and though annoyed with Paris, are not prepared to fight. It is waste of time to tell them that if Communism triumphs in the capital anarchy will spread all over the country. They are too busy with their own problems.

In spite of this a few volunteers are expected from the Haute-Garonne to-day. M. Thiers has told the Assembly that the insurrection must be quelled by the end of the week. I am afraid he is over-optimistic.

The people of the Commune announced yesterday that our army had been cut in half by Flourens, and that Versailles was surrounded. In order to celebrate these victories, which are no more than wishful thinking, Paris was illuminated last night.

6th April 1871. We nearly had a Cabinet crisis yesterday!

The Right wing, eager to prepare the ground for the coming elections, proposed to remove all provincial mayors appointed either by Napoleon III or by the Revolutionary Defence Government, replacing them with men of their own choice. They also suggested dissolving the municipal councils.

M. Thiers, foreseeing that so severe a measure would jeo-
pardize his friendly relations with the Left, arranged for Baron
de Larcy to propose a compromise bill, acceptable to both parties,
but though a ministerial crisis was averted the quarrel has left a
good deal of bitter feeling.

The military governor of Marseilles telegraphed an urgent
request for more police to deal with disorders in the port last
night.

7th April 1871. M. Thiers is sending telegrams to all the
prefects and military governors in France for reinforcements.
Five thousand provincial troops have arrived since Monday.
Germany is releasing many officers and men from internment
camps, and these are being incorporated into the regiments we
are forming at Versailles. The survivors of the Imperial Guard
will form a special regiment, in which M. Thiers places great hope.

The organization of our army is a lengthy and difficult business. Meanwhile the Commune is shooting innocent citizens,
and looting shops and private houses. Neither our supporters
in Paris nor our friends in the provinces understand why the
army of Versailles is taking so long to be organized. They
point out that after six days' fighting we have not yet driven the
insurgents from the suburbs of Paris.

After a great deal of hesitation Marshal MacMahon has
accepted the post of Commander-in-Chief of the army of Versailles. He lacks initiative and energy, but has been chosen
because of the moral authority he undoubtedly exercises over
the army.

Fighting was intense at Neuilly yesterday. The insurgents,
who were ambushed in private houses, kept up incessant fire.
There is no doubt that those people are fighting with furious
determination. At one time, however, they were pushed back
beyond the bridge of Neuilly while our guns swept the avenue
de la Grande Armée.

The storming of the capital cannot take place until next week
at the earliest.

8th April 1871. Troops left Versailles during the night to relieve others who had fought all day. We are expecting to occupy the Porte de Maillot on the perimeter of Paris to-day.

As soon as M. Thiers and Marshal MacMahon are ready to storm the capital our machine-guns will sweep the insurgents from the western approaches. This morning Mont-Valérien started to bombard the Bois de Boulogne and the walls of the city.

A few loyal staff officers, caught in Paris, plan to seize La Muette, where they will rally the National Guards of Auteuil and Passy, who are eager to come over to our side. They may even be able to bring us several battalions from the centre of the city.

M. Thiers says:

'Be patient for another three days and you will have lost nothing by waiting.'

General Péchaud was killed yesterday at the bridge of Neuilly, and his aide-de-camp, wounded in both legs, is on the danger list.

10th April 1871. During the last two days our military operations have been confined to some gunfire, mostly from Mont-Valérien.

We have made no advance since the capture of the bridge of Neuilly, and no major operation is scheduled for to-day.

Marshal MacMahon is planning his attack on Paris. Conferences are taking place at staff headquarters, and the offensive is to be resumed in the middle of next week.

M. Thiers denies the news, published in the *Gaulois*, that Bismarck has fixed 14th April as the date when the army of Versailles must beat the insurgents, failing which the Prussians will do so themselves. The Cabinet is of the opinion that Bismarck is only too happy to see us faced with this grave problem.

The officers commanding the National Guard of the Seine, though loyal to M. Thiers, are unable to escape from Paris. They have promised to rally their men as soon as our army enters

Paris, and, to distinguish these loyal troops from the rebels, we are making 10,000 armlets.

Considerable forces left Versailles to-day to take up positions designated by Marshal MacMahon.

11th April 1871. In the hope of appeasing the city of Paris, an article appeared in the *Journal Officiel* yesterday suggesting a pact between the Cabinet and the National Assembly to confirm the Republic.

As you can imagine, this statement caused intense indignation amongst the Royalist majority. I learn that it was not written by M. Thiers, but by M. Ernest Picard. These conflicting views within the Cabinet may soon produce serious consequences.

The Commune intends to pull down the famous column in the Place Vendôme because 'it symbolizes brute force, is an affirmation of militarism, and a negation of international rights.'

The monument is in honour of Napoleon's grand army, and is surmounted by a statue of Napoleon as a Roman Caesar. The cast bronze comes from guns captured in 1805.

Thiers gave no hope of a rapid advance of our troops into Paris when the Cabinet met last night, but Marshal MacMahon is expected to start his offensive to-morrow. Railroad employees, especially engine drivers, are being closely watched. They are suspected of intelligence with the enemy. An engine driver of the Lyons Railroad Company was arrested yesterday when trying to raise soldiers for the Commune.

14th April 1871. I have been away for two days, but on my return to Versailles I find the military and political situations unchanged. We have made no headway against the insurgents, and our military leaders warn us to expect no news for at least a week.

I passed through Nantes on 12th April, where I came across a train load of artillery (shells, powder, and twelve siege pieces) destined for Versailles. At 8 o'clock the next morning I was at Rouen, where I saw General von Fabrice, the Prussian commander, leaving Rouen, with all his senior officers, to establish new headquarters at Soisy, near Montmorency. I also saw a number of Prussian batteries leaving for the same destination.

General von Fabrice and his staff have no confidence in our military operations against the Communists. They claim that these operations are too slow, are lacking drive, and that they are likely to last beyond what the Germans call their 'patience.' The concentrations of German troops and material so near to Saint-Denis, and the arrival at Soisy of General von Fabrice, suggest that the German High Command is preparing to intervene if the Versailles Government is unable to force a decisive victory.

The Germans claim that our Cabinet will show itself as weak after victory as it is in achieving it.

'If M. Thiers merely shoots a dozen Anarchist leaders and pardons the rest, another revolution will flare up in less than a year,' they say.

Many workmen at Rouen have been on strike during the German occupation. There was an abortive attempt to set up a Commune.

15th April 1871. The heavy bombardment that lasted from 8 a.m. to 10 p.m. yesterday caused considerable casualties amongst our troops.

M. Thiers, at to-day's Cabinet meeting, gave little hope of a speedy victory, and appeared nervous and discouraged.

The resistance in Paris is increasing unrest in the provinces, where the Democratic party is still strong. This is specially the case at Lyons, Marseilles, Bordeaux, and Toulon.

The War Minister has been warned to keep a close watch on the 24th regiment of infantry before sending it to the front. This regiment, which arrived at Versailles on 13th April, was greatly undermined by propaganda of the Internationale at Cambrai. Another result of the resistance in Paris is to cause despondency amongst people in Alsace and Lorraine, who feel that if the Versailles Cabinet is unable to curb the insurrection, they will be forced to seek greater security under Prussian domination.

18th April 1871. M. Thiers is depressed, and though normally an amusing conversationalist, now keeps his own counsel. Reinforcements of 7,000 men are expected at Versailles on Thursday, and the War Minister says that in a week's time we shall have 120,000 men for an attack on Paris. The military experts are completing their plans for this operation, and M. Thiers's agents inside Paris are trying to bribe a number of rebel leaders to come over to us as soon as we force an entry.

The Communards are fighting blindly. They lean out of windows brandishing their rifles and shouting: 'We will conquer or die!'

Our army is impressed by this fanaticism and, tired by eight months of war, or weakened by internment in prison camps, it is in danger of losing its morale. Many officers say: 'If we have to die, let us be killed as soon as possible.'

The Commune has just dissolved the International Society for the Wounded on the grounds that it maintained intelligence with the enemy.

19th April 1871. General Ducrot is expected at Versailles to-morrow with a fresh division. We are to attack Paris within the next few days, and the plan is to occupy a section of the city —the Champs-Élysées, for example—and to make it our head-quarters while rallying loyal troops to our side.

20th April 1871. The parliamentary majority in the National Assembly is very discouraged, and appears appalled by its impotence, but it has no leader.

The Commune yesterday ordered the pillage of the Paris home of Marshal MacMahon in the rue Bellechasse. Removal vans took away all the furniture.

22nd April 1871. The marshal outlined his plan to occupy a district of Paris before a War Council presided over by M. Thiers yesterday. He is very anxious to avoid bloodshed and street fighting, and thinks that the best way of doing this is to bombard

F

sections occupied by the insurgents until they suffer such heavy casualties that they agree to lay down arms.

In the Champs-Élysées 400 torpedoes are connected by wires. Land mines are laid every 200 yards under the avenue de la Grande Armée. A trench filled with petroleum runs from the square in front of the Palais-Royal, connecting the rue de Castiglione and the rue de Rivoli with the mined barricade of the rue Saint-Florentin. Torpedoes have been placed under the Ministry of Marine and the Crillon.

There are also 200 mines under the rue de Castiglione. Engineers tunnelled under the terraces of the Tuileries and the rue des Capucines to put them there, and they endanger the entire heart of Paris from the river Seine to the boulevards, and from the Place de la Concorde to the Palais-Royal.

The Commune built hoardings to hide the work while laying the mines. These were removed as soon as the tunnelling was finished.

The Zouaves are leaving Versailles to-day for Toulon, where they will embark for Algeria to fight insurrections there.

25th April 1871. Our army is becoming impatient. The men are fighting bravely but with resignation, for they are longing to return to their native provinces and to their own families.

Since dawn our artillery has been bombarding the fort of Issy, which must be silenced before we can control the ramparts as far as the Porte Maillot.

26th April 1871. An emissary I sent to Paris tells me, on his return, that the National Guard is discouraged. The battalions returning from the battlefield drag themselves miserably through the streets while the population watches them sadly and in silence. The price of food is soaring and money is scarce.

Regular orgies are held at the War Office and the Hotel de Ville. These feasts produce scenes of unbridled revelry. Having stolen the cash reserves of the Paris Gas Company, the Commune intends to appropriate the bank balance of the water company.

3rd May 1871. An incident took place on the Paris boulevards two nights ago that shows some reaction against the reign of terror. A detachment of the National Guard, returning from the front, passed along shouting: 'Long live the Commune! Long live the Republic!'

Suddenly many people in the crowd answered: 'Long live Versailles!'

A number of youths are leaving Paris with forged passports. Apart from the rebels, only old men, women, and children are left in the capital.

4th May 1871. Twenty-five thousand of our picked troops camped in the Bois de Boulogne two nights ago. They were waiting for a pre-arranged signal to enter Paris. This signal was to have come from within; for M. Thiers, as I have told you, has a number of secret agents who travel between Versailles and Paris to bribe the chiefs of the Commune and battalion commanders.

Marshal MacMahon waited all night for the signal which was to open the gates of Paris, but nothing happened. Either our agents were unable to succeed or else they were caught.

The marshal returned to Versailles at 4 a.m. without achieving anything.

11th May 1871. After the meeting of the National Assembly yesterday M. Thiers went to Montretout to watch our batteries firing. He returned to the Prefecture to attend an important dinner, at which he talked with a number of deputies.

M. Thiers said that our entry into Paris was now only a matter of days, and that he is certain that our army will be received enthusiastically by most of the population. He confirmed that Bismarck intended sending German troops to Paris, but said that the chancellor had changed his mind.

M. Thiers believes that as soon as his troops capture Paris business will recover with a speed that will surprise everybody. Orders are already arriving from all parts of the world, and there are enough unfulfilled orders in Lyons and other industrial centres to keep factories busy for at least eighteen months.

13th May 1871. A fresh attempt was made during the night to enter Paris. Once again help was to come from within and, in fact, one of the gates was opened, but as soon as the first column started to pass through it was met by a rain of machine-gun bullets.

We shall probably be obliged to take the city by direct assault.

15th May 1871. I sent one of my agents to Paris yesterday. He returned to Versailles this morning with the news that our capture of Vanves has caused dissension in the ranks of the insurrectional committees and the National Guard. Besly, one of the hotheads of the Commune, has resigned. The Commune is losing ground in the suburbs of Vaugirard, Grenelle, and Alma. These suburbs refuse to go on fighting, and the women, who some time ago excited their husbands to combat, now urge them to lay down arms. The War Ministry made another attempt yesterday to rally the National Guard near the Bank of France, but failed because of the hostility of the Paris crowds.

Three hundred National Guards who went on strike were imprisoned by the Reds in the church of Notre-Dame-de-Lorette yesterday. A battalion which received orders to attack Auteuil on the 13th gave itself up, with its officers, to our troops.

The first of our regiments to enter Paris will be welcomed with open arms by the majority of the population, and the 15,000 or 20,000 Anarchists who threaten to blow up Paris will not be strong enough to continue the struggle.

The Paris Omnibus Company has only enough oats for a week. Every day this company spends 30,000 francs more than its revenue, and its vehicles are being requisitioned at the rate of eighty a day. The insurrection is near its end.

The National Assembly debated the peace treaty in its final form at Versailles yesterday. The deputies, knowing that the articles of the treaty could not be modified, decided to ratify it without discussion. There are times when silence is another word for dignity.

19th May 1871. We are at peace with Germany.

Now we must make peace at home.

Several incidents took place during the last stages of the debate on the ratification of the treaty which show what violent antagonism can break out between Royalists and Republicans at the slightest provocation.

M. Favre was summoned to Frankfort by Bismarck yesterday. The reason for his visit is a slight rectification of the frontier near Belfort.

24th May 1871. Paris has fallen.

M. Thiers is now faced with his most difficult task—that of reorganizing France and choosing a permanent regime.

A violent controversy is raging:

1. To proclaim a Republic.
2. To proclaim a Monarchy.
3. To maintain the *status quo.*

The first solution is backed by the Left, but has no chance of being adopted by the National Assembly so long as the majority remains staunchly Monarchist.

[Between this letter and the next the insurgents fired many of the most historic buildings and churches in Paris. Firemen who tried to extinguish the flames were shot.

Incendiaries threw cans and bottles filled with petroleum, phosphorus, nitro-glycerine, and other explosives into the cellars. Men and women were offered ten francs for each house that was destroyed.

The Tuileries, home of the kings of France, dating from 1564, was fired on the night of the 23rd. The following morning columns of smoke rose above Paris, so thick that the sun was blotted out. Fires raged in the Hôtel de Ville, the Palais-Royal, the Ministry of Finance, the Prefecture of Police, the Palais de Justice, the Conseil d'État; in the rue de Lille, the rue du Bac, the Faubourgs Saint-Germain and Saint-Honoré, and the rue Royale. By Friday night the docks and warehouses were ablaze; mines and torpedoes were exploding. So fierce were the flames that a newspaper could be read by their light as far away as Versailles!

The Tuileries burned for three days and three nights; ten days afterwards the ruins blazed forth again. Millions of pounds' worth of works of art were destroyed in less than a week. The Gobelins school of tapestry was destroyed in spite of the heroic efforts of the employees. The army of Versailles entered a city of desolation.]

X. THIERS—PRESIDENT OF THE REPUBLIC

VERSAILLES, *30th May 1871*. I have spoken with influential members of the parliamentary majority who claim that the retirement of M. Jules Favre and M. Ernest Picard from the Government will not prove sufficient to avert a crisis. These two politicians believed that M. Thiers would observe the Bordeaux pact whereby all Cabinet ministers agreed to stand or fall together.

But M. Thiers has assumed the powers of an absolute monarch, and his critics call him Adolphe I.

The laws of exile against the members of the Bonaparte family have lapsed. They could be renewed by the National Assembly, but this is most unlikely. Nevertheless, if Napoleon III or his ministers were to return to France, many deputies would insist on their immediate arrest for treason, and they would be deported.

Paris, 12th June 1871. The postal services from Versailles are so irregular and so delayed that I have returned to Paris.

Everything is being organized, or rather disorganized, at Versailles to oblige the National Assembly to come back to the capital. Ministers claim that their departments cannot function so long as half the administrative offices are at Versailles and the other half in Paris. If M. Thiers wished to make Versailles the capital he ought first of all to have left the headquarters of the postal and telegraph service there. Versailles is now very late in keeping up communications with the provinces and abroad.

M. Thiers would like the National Assembly to leave Versailles as a sign of goodwill towards Paris as soon as the elections have taken place.

The presence of the Prince and Princesse de Joinville and the Duc d'Aumale at Versailles has done much to bring the two Monarchist parties together. The principal members of the Legitimist party have visited these two Orleanist princes. The Prince de Joinville is very deaf, and it was the Duc d'Aumale who generally spoke. He is gay and affable, and is very grateful for being allowed to remain on French soil. He appears to have no personal ambitions, and he will only play a major role if it is thrust upon him.

M. Grévy, President of the National Assembly, is living at Versailles.

He occupies the apartments of Louis XIV, so that our Republican president received the two royal princes in the apartment of their ancestors.

Our Minister of Finance occupies the small apartments of Louis XIV.

Baron de Larcy, Minister of Public Works, occupies the apartments of Mme Du Barry.

The Minister of Commerce, the Republican Victor Lefranc, lives in the apartments of Mme de Maintenon!

1st July 1871. I am just back from Versailles, where I gathered the following news.

The Prince of Joinville called on the Marquis de la Ferté, the Comte de Chambord's representative at Versailles, to ask him, on behalf of his nephew, the Comte de Paris, when he could pay his respects to the head of the house of Bourbon.

The Prince de Joinville introduced himself as Colonel Lutteroth, the name he assumed when serving in the army of the Loire under General Chanzy.

The Marquis de la Ferté said that he would advise the Comte de Chambord immediately of the Comte de Paris's request, and as the Comte de Chambord was close to the frontier, he hoped to have an answer at the latest to-morrow, Sunday. When the Comte de Paris expressed a wish to be received between the 2nd and the 10th July the Marquis de la Ferté answered that, as

M. Thiers

M. le Comte de Paris's visit was expected, the Comte de Chambord would certainly arrange a meeting with his cousin as speedily as possible.

The parliamentary majority in the National Assembly is very excited about this. The Comte de Paris will be accompanied by his brother, the Duc de Chartres.

The princes have declared they will impose no conditions for their reconciliation with the head of their house.

There is no longer any doubt, therefore, that this visit will take place early next week. This is a very important fact, because, by bringing to an end the divisions in the house of Bourbon, a re-establishment of the monarchy becomes much easier when the moment is propitious. It is important to note that what is known as the 'fusion' between the Orleanists and the Legitimists was made at Bordeaux and at Versailles before the princes of Orleans decided to reconcile themselves with the head of their house. The Comte de Paris yesterday visited several ministers, notably the Baron de Larcy. This evening the young prince dines with M. Thiers. In spite of all this politeness, the princes and the Monarchist parties bear a big grudge against M. Thiers for all his efforts to retain the Republic. The results of the elections will decide if the truce is to be prolonged or if the Royalist majority will engage itself in a struggle against M. Thiers. For the moment M. Thiers is the stronger.

3rd July 1871. The elections, which are partial, took place quietly. There are 111 deputies to be elected. Of these, twenty-one are for the department of the Seine [Paris and its outer suburbs], and the remainder for forty-six provincial departments.

Most of the Republican electors in Paris abstained. On the other hand, the middle classes, terrified by the Commune, rushed to the polls and voted Conservative.

The final results will be known to-morrow night.

Provincial voting is causing surprise.

Out of twenty-one departments, where results are known,

fourteen returned Republicans. A notable exception is the department of the Rhône [including the city of Lyons], which has voted Conservative.

General Faidherbe, who commanded the army of the north, has been elected. So has Gambetta. The Bonapartists have elected M. Pierre Magne, a former minister of Napoleon III, and M. de Soubeyran.

4th July 1871. Last February the provinces voted Conservative and Monarchist, and Paris voted Anarchist. This time Paris has voted Conservative, and the provinces Republican!

I have often stressed M. Thiers's secret alliance with the Left. This alliance was chiefly marked by the understanding between our chief executive and the delegates of the Paris municipal councils during the Commune. It proved that M. Thiers's personal sympathies favoured the preservation of the Republic at all costs.

The elections will strengthen the Republican party in the National Assembly by about 100 members, who will uphold M. Thiers against the Monarchists, but the Conservative majority, though smaller, still exceeds 400 votes.

11th July 1871. Following the manifesto of the Comte de Chambord, the Legitimists in the National Assembly are divided as to what they should do. Some talk of resigning and returning to private life; others of prolonging the powers of M. Thiers and of rallying themselves to the Republic; but most of them are of the opinion that it is wisest to do nothing; it is this point of view that is likely to prevail. All the Legitimists in the Assembly persist in remaining united with the Orleanists in order that the Conservative majority should not be broken. This majority is essential for the interests of the country in the present circumstances.

The maintenance of this accord appears all the more necessary because M. Thiers is no longer a young man and anything might happen to him. Last evening at Versailles, in one of the principal *salons* where members of the majority were to be found, the conversation turned on the revelations of a scandal sheet alleging that M. Thiers is visiting a lady in Paris more often than is wise for a gentleman of seventy-four. It was even suggested that our chief executive had a stroke during a visit three weeks ago. M. Thiers's supporters are very indignant, and say that women are not one of his failings. Outside the Assembly the Comte de Chambord's manifesto has caused a division of opinion among the Legitimists in Paris and in the provinces; some Monarchist newspapers write in support of the part of the manifesto relative to the white flag;[1] others write against it.

12th July 1871. Friends of the Orleanist princes suggested a few days ago that the Comte de Paris should publish a counter-manifesto in favour of retaining the tricolour in order to offset the Comte de Chambord's manifesto. The idea was abandoned for fear of splitting the Conservative party at the very moment when the Bonapartists and the Republicans are conspiring for power.

Although the Orleanist princes have cancelled their meeting with the Comte de Chambord they remain faithful to their pledge recognizing him as the head of the House of Bourbon.

The Constitutional Legitimists, those who favoured the Comte de Chambord personally, and who have stepped aside, say that since his manifesto he has taken the position of Henri IV *before the mass*.[2] They add that the Comte de Paris, in recognizing

---

[1] The manifesto, made known on 5th July following the Comte de Chambord's dramatic return to Paris, included these words relative to his flag:

'Frenchmen, I am amongst you.

'You have opened the doors of France to me, and I could not resist the happiness of seeing my country again.

'I am ready to do anything to help my country rise from its ruins and regain its rightful place in the world. The only sacrifice I refuse to make is that of my honour.

'I will not allow anybody to take away from me the standard of Henri IV, of François Ier, and of Jeanne d'Arc. The white flag of the kings of France flew above my cradle at birth; it is my will that it shall shade my tomb after death. Henri V cannot and will not abandon the flag of Henri IV.'

[2] Henri IV abjured Protestantism to become King of France. 'Paris vaut bien une messe.'—'Paris is well worth a mass.'

the principle of hereditary monarchy in the person of the Comte de Chambord, has become the Dauphin, that is to say, the direct heir, in case of abdication or the death of the Comte de Chambord.

Arrests continue to be made in Paris against the vandals and murderers of the Commune. Over 25,000 already await trial, and this number will doubtless be considerably increased. An old woman who deals in bric-à-brac has just been arrested in the Passage de l'Opéra. She is accused of receiving stolen objects from M. Thiers's Paris house, pillaged during the Commune. Her name is Mme Alexandre. She is said to have been a beauty in her day, and to have attracted the Duc d'Orléans, father of the Comte de Paris.

13th July 1871. The editor of the *Revue des Deux Mondes*, who was received in London some time ago by the Comte de Paris, went to see him in Paris yesterday, asking for precise facts about his reconciliation with the head of the house of Bourbon.

The Comte de Paris discussed the Comte de Chambord's recent manifesto, and said:

'It is not we Orleanists, but the public, who oppose the white flag. Our feelings towards M. le Comte de Chambord remain unchanged and continue to be most cordial. Great tact is necessary at this juncture, but there is no hurry to force an issue, because we have to deal with M. Thiers, who is making an experiment with the Republic. I ask you therefore to hold up your article.'

The Duc de Nemours says the same thing.

I would like you to bear this in mind, because there is no question of the Orleanists seizing the throne, as Louis-Philippe did in 1830.

Marshal MacMahon, who is to be Commander-in-Chief of the entire French army, insists that General Ladmirault should be military governor of Paris, because, says the marshal, 'I must be sure of my man.'

General Ladmirault, commanding the first army corps, was

one of the first to enter Paris during the Commune. He led his
men in by the Porte d'Auteuil, and took up strong positions
in the streets of Passy.

Many more arrests were made to-day, especially near the
Bourse. The Communards are in a state of terror. The police
and the military swear that not a single leader will escape.

17th July 1871. M. Walewski and twenty-four deputies are to
propose the immediate transfer of the National Assembly to
Paris. The Conservative majority, however, appears to be in
no hurry to leave Versailles. I believe that the Assembly will
suspend its sittings from 15th August until 15th September,
when it must meet again to draft the budget.

The Comtesse Walewska,[1] who, during the siege of Paris
and the Commune, spent most of the time at the Château des
Ornano in the Touraine, has arrived in Paris.

Mme Walewska called on M. Thiers at Versailles yesterday on
behalf of her son, Charles Walewski, and her future son-in-law,
M. de Bourgueney. Charles Walewski does not want to be an
attaché at Vienna under the Marquis de Banneville, but would
prefer to be sent to Japan. Mlle Élise Walewska is to marry
M. de Bourgueney, who is also to enter the diplomatic service.

[1] Her husband, Comte Alexandre Colonna Walewski, who died in 1867,
was a natural son of Napoleon I and the Polish Comtesse Marie Walewska.
He was the French ambassador in London in 1852, and it was greatly due to
him that Great Britain recognized Napoleon III.

On his return to France he became Foreign Minister, but his views, diametrically opposed to the Nationalist principles of Napoleon III, led to an
angry tilt with the emperor during the Italian negotiations in 1859.

The Prince de la Tour d'Auvergne, French Minister in Turin, having
received instructions from Comte Walewski, called with them on Cavour,
who exclaimed ironically: 'I have received a letter, direct from your emperor,
telling me not to worry.'

Mme Walewska, by her delicate diplomacy, helped to restore good
relations between her husband and Napoleon III. A Florentine by birth,
her illustrious family could be traced back to Machiavelli. Fresh and fair
as March corn, with lively grey-blue eyes and delicate features, she was
described by Mme Adélaïde, sister of Louis-Philippe, in these words:

'This young woman is seductive. She is more than beautiful because
she has the charm of simplicity.'

Though Mme Walewska no longer enjoys the privileges of an imperial court she continues to live in grand style. She is still very beautiful.

18th July 1871. Our ministers at Versailles are complaining more and more about M. Thiers's domineering character.

He, who during his long career has not ceased to attack all forms of personal government, has become the most personal government ever known. His ministers complain that not one of them is able to take any decision without having consulted M. Thiers, and that he always claims to know more about a question than the minister concerned. In this he is probably often right.

M. Pouyer-Quertier, the Minister of Finance, complains more bitterly than anybody of M. Thiers's omnipotence. It is a known fact that our illustrious elder statesman believes that he has unrivalled knowledge of finance and military questions.

Comte Walewski used to tell a story about M. Thiers to illustrate this.

At one time Comte Walewski intended to marry Mlle Félicie, Mme Thiers's sister. One day, at the Thierses' home, the conversation turned on horses, and the count was telling his fiancée about his hunters, when M. Thiers suddenly broke in and made a long speech, the tenor of which was that Comte Walewski did not know the first thing about a horse. On his way home that night Comte Walewski reflected that if he married into the family of a man who showed such contempt for the knowledge of others, he would be obliged to play a very minor role.

He therefore decided not to marry Mlle Félicie, who has remained a spinster to this day.

The Comte de Falloux is back in Paris from Versailles, where he spent a fortnight. Invited to M. Thiers's home one evening last week, M. de Falloux upbraided our chief executive for brushing aside the Bordeaux agreement; for his criminal weakness in flirting with the delegates of the Paris municipal councils during the Commune; for his opposition to the parliamentary system;

and for the way he has chosen his ministers from outside the Conservative majority of the National Assembly.

M. Thiers lost his temper, and turning his back on the learned academician, exclaimed:

'You 're a fanatic!'

The next day M. Thiers, shamefaced and eager to atone for his bad behaviour, invited M. de Falloux to dinner.

20th July 1871. A friend of mine, a leading physician, who is also a friend of M. Thiers, went to see our chief executive at Versailles yesterday. He found him suffering from such a severe attack of bronchitis that he will not be able to attend the Budget Committee. He is tired and longing for a rest.

M. Pierre Magne [former minister of Napoleon III], who is still on very good terms with M. Thiers, confirmed what my physician said, and added that M. Thiers was seriously thinking about a successor. I met M. Magne in Mme Walewska's *salon.* The former Minister of Finance does not believe that the Bonapartists have any chance of coming back, and I found him much more concerned about the growing Communist propaganda in the provinces. He blamed the Government for not disbanding the National Guard, but said that he would support M. Thiers as long as he can remain in power.

Mme Walewska is going to spend a short holiday at Dieppe, and has taken a fine apartment in one of the hotels overlooking the sea.

The Bourse is quietly firm. The business recovery is being retarded by a lack of skilled men in industry, and by the difficulties of hauling raw materials by railroad.

22nd July 1871. Friction between the parliamentary majority and the Cabinet, which was noticeable once more during yesterday's debate in the Chamber, is due to the Monarchist views of the majority and the Republican views of M. Thiers and his Cabinet. This mutual distrust is augmented by the fact that, contrary to constitutional principles, most of M. Thiers's colleagues were chosen from outside the majority. This explains why, in spite of the pact signed at Bordeaux, this incompatibility breaks out between the majority and the Government at every moment. So far a break has been avoided, but it can take place on the day one least expects it.

M. Thiers has sent a telegram to the German emperor thanking him for his decision to evacuate immediately the departments of the Eure, the Somme, and the Seine-Inférieure.

We received news from M. Chaumont, our financial agent in Strasburg, to the effect that the Germans were retarding our payments of 500,000,000 francs of war indemnity because of their unwillingness to hasten the counting of the money.

Two days ago the German authorities sent seventeen officials to count our gold, but they were unable to deal with more than 700,000 francs a day.

M. Chaumont urged the Germans to send more officials, so that the settlement could be expedited, thus freeing our territory, but the Germans refused. M. Thiers has now sent a personal telegram to the emperor, who has promised to take the matter up.

25th July 1871. You will have noticed how the Conservative majority in the Chamber votes solidly together on every important issue, not only against the Left, but also in committee and against M. Thiers and his ministers.

In talking during the last few days with the chief members of this majority, I find them very decided on these three points:

1. To keep and formally establish the Government and the National Assembly at Versailles.

2. To constitute a Cabinet which is representative of the majority.

3. To demobilize all the National Guards.

M. Thiers has already been obliged by the majority to drop M. Ernest Picard from his Cabinet. Following Saturday's vote it is now the turn of M. Jules Favre. It will not be long before M. Jules Simon follows, and the same thing applies to M.

Dufaure, who shows himself too well disposed towards the Republican magistrature.

Thus M. Thiers, in spite of his relations with the Left, will therefore find himself more and more ringed in by a ministry of the Right. The majority leaders want to make M. Moulin a member of the Cabinet. He is president of the extra-parliamentary reunion of the Right.

As for the third point in the majority's programme, the majority insists upon it in spite of M. Thiers, who claims that the dissolution of the National Guard would lead to civil war.

The members of the majority answer that, far from this, it is the maintenance of the National Guards that is leading us inevitably to a civil war, and the Government is making the same mistake which led to the disaster and the crimes of the Commune. Deputies are receiving information from the provinces which leaves no doubt about the propaganda of the Communards, who are relying on the National Guard to avenge their defeat in Paris. These deputies add that M. Thiers is most unwise to provide arms for future insurrections.

26th July 1871. The chief executive stubbornly refuses to drop his Cabinet colleagues of the 4th September revolution. This cannot fail to widen the breach between him and his parliamentary majority, and cause a conflict. He is in disagreement with the majority on all the chief questions of political, administrative, military, and financial reorganization.

Deputies continue to receive letters from the provinces saying that the Demagogues, encouraged by the slackness and indecision of the Government, are becoming more aggressive.

The Bishop of Orleans, whose last speech was so eulogistic of M. Thiers, said to a group of deputies yesterday:

'M. Thiers, after saving us, is leading us to disaster.'

Though the red flag no longer flies at Lyons, the Red party is still very menacing, and the inhabitants do not yet dare to unseal their cellars for fear of incendiaries.

Prince Napoleon is said to have made a second attempt to land in France—this time at Le Havre; but he was sent back.

The wedding of Mlle Élise Walewska to M. de Bourgueney is to take place in October; the bridegroom is to be an attaché at our embassy in Washington.

M. Alexandre Walewski, consul at Alicante, whose mother was the celebrated tragedienne Rachel, is in Paris.

28th July 1871. The Government is keeping a close watch on the Bonapartists, whose agents are making too frequent journeys between this country and England.

There is a plot to land Louis-Napoleon at Rochefort during the parliamentary holiday next month. This port has been chosen because the people in the department of the Charente-Inférieure are particularly favourable to the former emperor.

The whole country would be asked to prove by a plebiscite its desire for a return of the Napoleonic dynasty.

This would argue that the army refused to remain faithful to the Republic; but the army has not forgotten Sedan and Metz.

It is said that the police are on the track of Félix Pyat,[1] who, unable to leave Paris, changes his lodgings and his disguise every day.

Surprise is caused by the way the Government allows the ex-Communard General La Cécilia[2] to wander about Paris just as he pleases.

29th July 1871. It appears far from certain that the latest attempt to prolong the powers of M. Thiers for a limited period will succeed. The majority criticizes M. Thiers's domineering influence, his refusal to draw up a parliamentary Cabinet, and his weakness in dealing with Demagogic propaganda in the

---

[1] In fact Pyat had fled to England. He was a fiery journalist, and a member of the Committee of Public Safety during the Commune.

[2] General La Cécilia's *prima donna*-like name belied his savagery.

provinces. It is therefore averse to granting him a fixed term of office. We must expect some lively debates, and, at all events, enough opposition to make M. Thiers's position less strong than it is now.

An official of the library of the Legislative Body is at the Palais-Bourbon in Paris to help deputies who find the parliamentary library at Versailles inadequate.

M. de Lavalette, founder of the newspaper *L'Assemblée Nationale*, suppressed under the Empire, but lately published in London, has arrived in Paris to produce the newspaper here. It will be the organ of the Royalist fusion—as it was in 1848.

31st July 1871. The results of the second ballot for the Paris municipal council shows that at least a dozen Radicals who played major roles during the Commune will figure in the final list. The National Assembly feels that this is full justification for it to remain at Versailles.

M. Thiers said yesterday that during the parliamentary holiday he would reorganize the army, and study the new frontiers caused by the loss of Alsace and Lorraine.

It is urgent to remove the remnants of our army from Paris. Agents are continually accosting soldiers, whom they invite into the cafés and wine shops, where they incite them to sedition. If our troops are left in the capital for another month we shall see a repetition of the Commune.

What a pity that Balzac, whose descriptions of modern vice were so brilliant, is dead.

Debauchery, which during the siege and the Commune was relatively latent, now appears to be making up for lost time. The police are swooping down on a number of lingerie and perfumery shops, notably in the Passage de l'Opéra. It is here that Mme Alexandre, the bric-à-brac dealer who was arrested some time ago for receiving stolen objects from M. Thiers's house when it was pillaged during the Commune, has some private rooms at the back of her shop where, on the excuse of showing elderly gentlemen her rarest treasures, she introduces them to ladies of easy virtue.

It was perhaps unwise to release her so quickly from jail.

The newspaper kiosks on the boulevards only sell newspapers as a blind. They are run by women who arrange their evening rendezvous. The kiosk numbered 246 in front of the Grand Hotel is in this category. It only opens in the afternoon. Kiosk No. 26, near the rue de Taitbout, is occupied by a woman who calls herself Comtesse de Courzon. The tobacco shop in the Passage de l'Opéra is owned by a Demoiselle Calémade de Lafayette, a niece of the deputy of the Haute-Loire!

2nd August 1871. Yesterday's debate in the Chamber again revealed that resolute and compact majority of 430 votes, which resists not only M. Thiers, but his ministers, and all sections of the Left.

Each time M. Thiers finds himself in conflict with the majority he uses his personal authority to shield his ministers, as was the case yesterday with M. Lambrecht, Minister of the Interior. This is in utter contradiction of the constitutional system, by which the ministers should shield the head of the State. The day will come when the majority of 430 will not hesitate to demand M. Thiers's resignation; the Conservatives are tired of his personal government, irritated by his flirtations with the Left wing, and more worried than ever by the Demagogic propaganda in the provinces.

As there is no hope that M. Thiers will change his politics, the majority will change M. Thiers.

The Bourse was lower for the reasons I have just outlined.

7th August 1871. The ovation given by the Chamber on Saturday to M. Buffet, the Monarchist, was a source of grave irritation to M. Thiers, who parried the blow by insisting on a vote of confidence. M. Thiers's tartness with M. Buffet is due to his conviction that this member, who undoubtedly exercises great influence with the majority, wants to step into his shoes.

M. Buffet does not spare M. Thiers his sharp wit. Referring the other day to our chief executive's impatience when contradicted, he said:

'I am surrounded at Versailles by portraits of Louis XIV, and if this monarch still lived I should probably find it easier to speak to him than to M. Thiers!'

The Comte de Bouillé, our ambassador in Madrid, has had a disagreeable adventure. He never smokes, whereas the young King of Spain is an inveterate smoker.

After dinner at the palace a few nights ago the king led the way to the smoking-room, where he started puffing at a powerful cigar. All the courtiers followed suit. The Comte de Bouillé, taken suddenly ill, was sick all over the august monarch!

Alas! This diplomat's presence in Madrid is no longer possible.

10th August 1871. The courts martial set up to judge the leaders of the Commune will be busy till the end of the year.

Most of the accused are so impertinent that the judges are not tempted to show great indulgence.

Assy gives himself the airs of a fop and a dandy. Each time he says a few words he coughs with affectation as if this effort hurt his chest. Then he pulls out a handkerchief and looks impudently at the public. His voice is quite unnatural; he tries to make it melodious.

[Assy was the burly ex-strike organizer of the Creusot works who gave himself the title of Colonel of the National Guards during the Commune, organized street barricades, became the most vociferous instigator of murder, incited the crowds to pillage M. Thiers's house, and was for a time governor of the Hôtel de Ville. He made incendiary shells filled with petroleum to fire national buildings in Paris.]

Ferré gives himself the airs of a Bohemian student whom the world has treated badly. He is unctuous and polite.

[Ferré visited the Archbishop of Paris in his cell during the Commune to tell him that his last hour had come.]

Colonel Merlin, the president of the court, is considered far too lenient—he is not the right man to conduct these trials.

The attitude of the accused men indicates that they feel themselves protected in high circles, and others will seek to imitate them unless exemplary sentences are passed.

Daumas, who yesterday had the impudence to make a seditious speech in the National Assembly, is Radical deputy for the Var.

14th August 1871. The majority is divided on the question of prolonging the powers of M. Thiers. Whereas a powerful section of the Right is inclined to oppose it, a fairly considerable group, headed by the Duc d'Audiffret Pasquier and M. de Broglie, and including most of the Fusionists, favour a compromise. The parliamentary commissaries are not willing to modify the Rivet [1] motion, but, on the contrary, seek to extend it by asking that a complete constitution should be drawn up within the scope of the Bordeaux pact. In this way the principle of the constitution, not the constitutional form of the Government, would be final. A basis would then be found whereby the Republic could ultimately be changed into a monarchy. The Left, which did not foresee the consequences of its action, now bitterly regrets having forced the Assembly to declare itself constituent.

25th August 1871. The difference of opinion that exists between M. Thiers and the parliamentary majority caused a violent scene in the National Assembly yesterday. M. Thiers became

---

[1] M. Rivet, a friend of M. Thiers, tabled a motion raising M. Thiers to the title of President of the Republic. M. Thiers was to continue exercising the functions he assumed on 17th February, but his powers were to be limited to three years. Gambetta opposed this motion, and wanted to form a constituent assembly.

excited and, at times, menacing, while the Conservatives, who interrupted him continually, roared defiance.

There is a moral divorce between the antagonists, but negotiations have been taking place during the night to prevent a separation in fact.

M. Thiers left the Chamber in such a state of agitation that Mme Thiers was extremely worried. Her husband told her at dinner that he was going to send his resignation to the president of the National Assembly, but Mme Thiers persuaded him to postpone it for twenty-four hours.

The Radicals are eager for M. Thiers to remain in power—at any rate until they have no more use for him. For this reason M. Thiers's Radical friends remained with him most of the night at the Prefecture. They want him to take advantage of the coming debates on the Rivet motion to ask for a vote of confidence.

[The National Assembly, having declared itself constituent by 434 votes to 225, bestowed the title of President of the French Republic on M. Thiers by 491 votes to 94.]

4th September 1871. The majority, before leaving Versailles, wants to draw up measures to counter M. Thiers's weakness with the Demagogues. Deputies are wondering if the President of the Republic is not dominated by fear because, having the support of the majority, it would be easy for him to act vigorously. He takes no steps to oppose the deliberations of the municipal councils or the open resistance of certain members of the National Guard to the dissolution of that body voted by the Assembly.

General Bourbaki has written to M. Thiers telling him that if he orders the dissolution of the National Guard at Lyons he will see that it is done within twenty-four hours without a shot being fired. M. Thiers has not answered.

[General Bourbaki was commander of the sixth army corps and military governor of Lyons.]

The majority, from what many deputies tell me, is most displeased about the sentences that the military court martial at Versailles is pronouncing against the leaders of the Commune. The president is considered far too lenient, especially in the case of Courbet, whose six months' imprisonment was hardly adequate for his crimes.[1] The army is also irritated at this light sentence, because many officers say that it is not fair to have asked them to risk their lives to put down the Commune if these murderers and incendiaries get off so lightly.

Versailles offers no recreation to our legislators. It amused me on Saturday to hear solemn Conservative deputies planning a Sunday outing at Suresnes, where they looked forward to attending a popular open-air ball, for which the entrance fee is four sous.

9th September 1871. Official reports draw attention to increasing Napoleonic propaganda in the provinces.

It is not without success, for many provincial people remember with pleasure the eighteen years of prosperity under the Second Empire, and they do not realize the price they paid for them.

The rural districts are being worked up, not only by the Bonapartists, but also by the Socialists of the Internationale. Some people see an affinity between the two regimes.

The information I have from the provinces leads me to suppose that if the Napoleonic party succeeded in calling a plebiscite, it would obtain between 5,000,000 and 6,000,000 votes. This is only 1,500,000 fewer than the emperor received in his tremendously successful plebiscite of 8th May 1870, when, just before the war with Germany, he wanted to make contact with his people and test their feelings towards him.[2]

Many people claim that Prince Bismarck would be glad to

---

[1] A painter of the ultra-realistic school, Courbet was appointed Director of the Beaux-Arts during the Commune. He played a leading role in the destruction of the Colonne Vendôme.

[2] Napoleon received 7,336,000 votes in his favour; there were 1,560,000 against him.

see Napoleon III return. I do not doubt it. The former emperor certainly did everything he could to deserve Prussian gratitude!

In the Paris *salons*, or what *salons* are left, you can well imagine that this question of a Bonapartist restoration—whether in favour of Napoleon III or of a regency—is the one subject of conversation.

Heavy taxation to meet the indemnity will make peasants increasingly antagonistic to the Republic.

11th September 1871. The agents of the Napoleonic regime place a great deal of hope in General Bourbaki and the regiments of what used to be the Imperial Guard.

General Bourbaki's sister, Mme Lebreton, lady-in-waiting to the Empress Eugénie, has followed her into exile and remains her confidante. It is therefore through the good offices of Mme Lebreton that the Bonapartists will seek to influence the general.

People are wondering what the Orleanist princes would do if Napoleon tried to stage a come-back. These princes, who are so happy to be back in France, would immediately be exiled if Napoleon succeeded. Yet how could they resist? Would they start a movement of their own, ally themselves to the Republicans, or fight under the banner of Henri V, head of the house of Bourbon?

Anything may happen. We are living under a Provisional Government, run by an old gentleman of seventy-four! He could disappear any day and then you would see the crisis—the crisis for which the Bonapartists want to be ready.

13th September 1871. When four newspapers, charged with exaggerating the Communist troubles at Lyons, were acquitted at the assize courts yesterday, several members of the jury went up to the journalists concerned and said to them:

'The Government should have prosecuted the Communists —not you!'

One juryman said that his family lived at Lyons, and that he knew that the dispatches published in these papers were absolutely true.

But M. Thiers refuses to be firm.

19th September 1871. The principal agents of the Bonapartist party are in Paris, and are very active. They have organized a central press bureau, manned by former directors of the Ministry of the Interior during the Second Empire. These people have been putting out stories about M. Thiers's ill health, but as it happens the president has seldom been so well.

20th September 1871. The home situation is flourishing.

The disarming of the National Guard is taking place without incident, and the Anarchists are thus deprived of an armed force. The Bonapartists have no following to speak of in the army, and the Ministry of Finance announces that taxes are coming in faster than anybody dared imagine. The reorganization of the army is going on apace.

25th September 1871. Information that reaches me from the provinces shows that our deputies have not been received with any great warmth in their constituencies.

The National Assembly, in its desire to be prudent and not to hasten the solution of any outstanding problem, has succeeded in displeasing both the Monarchists and the Republicans.

M. Thiers's eclectic policy, on the other hand, appears to suit a nation which during the last eighty years has passed through so many different regimes.

20th October 1871. One of the emperor's followers, who was with him during his first two attempts to seize power—at Strasburg in 1836, and at Boulogne in 1840—has just been to see him in England.

He found the emperor exhausted, both mentally and physically. When asked what plans he had for regaining the throne Napoleon answered that even if the army revolted in his favour he would not return unless called by a plebiscite.

When reminded of Strasburg and Boulogne the emperor said:

'Those are the things one does in youth. I am neither able nor willing to attempt a *coup d'état.*'

I do not know whether these are Napoleon's true sentiments, but they have come as a bitter blow to his partisans in France, who remain very ardent. There is a club in the Boulevard des Capucines (known to Bonapartists as the Boulevard de l'Île d'Elbe) called the Intimidation Club. Its members intend, when the right times comes, to publish documents to compromise the neo-Republicans who once served the emperor.

M. Ferry was to have left Marseilles for Ajaccio on the 17th, but as the ship in which he was to cross was called *Prince Napoléon*, he decided to wait till the end of the week, when he could sail on the *Insulaire*.

25th October 1871. I am back in Paris after a short tour of the European courts, where I was able to obtain some idea of what people are thinking about France.

In general I found that M. Thiers is considered prudent and intelligent, but people say that his policy of seesawing between the Right and the Left is not sufficient to replace a real constitutional Government.

There is no lack of sympathy for us abroad, and Europe as a whole realizes that its own destiny is tied up with ours. Indeed, there is everywhere a certainty that we shall rise again stronger than ever.

Except amongst a few classes in England nobody has any faith in the Napoleonic regime, or any regrets about its disappearance.

Communist exiles abroad are keeping up a close correspondence with the Radical party here.

PS. There was a great explosion of optimism on the Bourse to-day.

27th October 1871. A former prefect and senator tells me that, with the aid of several colleagues, he has just completed statistics to show how the four chief political parties would stand if a free plebiscite were to be held at the present time.

This is his guess:

Three million people would vote for the Napoleonic regime.

Two million for the Republic.

Two million for a Bourbon king.

One million for an Orleanist king.

There is nothing improbable in these figures.

Many former civil servants, senators, secretaries, and ministers of state who believed the Second Empire eternal are to-day in varying degrees of poverty. One sees, for instance, the former Senator Comte de Flammarens wandering in the Batignolles district dressed like a beggar.

A former judge of the high court asked a factory owner the other day for a minor secretarial position.

These unfortunate people are naturally hoping for a return of the Napoleonic dynasty.

M. Thiers received a deputation from the Conseil Général of the Seine-et-Oise yesterday. He renewed his promise not to do anything against the Republic, and he urged every good patriot to rally to the cause and not to compromise the regime by any act of violence.

This advice, which conforms with everything that M. Thiers has said since his arrival at Versailles, is considered by his opponents as a violation of the strict neutrality he agreed to keep at Bordeaux.

But M. Thiers says that because of the inaction of the Monarchist parties he is now at liberty to take sides with the Republic.

Meanwhile the *Figaro* criticizes the Comte de Chambord for not appearing in public and for remaining outside French territory in a solitude which it describes as 'mysterious and inaccessible.'

I ought to add that this article of the *Figaro* echoes the discontent shown by most of the Legitimists, who claim that the Comte de Chambord is counting too much on a miracle for the return of this throne.

Because of all this M. Thiers and his followers remain masters of the situation, and can easily succeed in founding a strong Republic.

4th November 1871. Our Foreign Minister told us at Versailles last night that the Comte de Chambord and King Leopold have sent a private communication to M. Thiers about the recent interview between the Emperor William and the Emperor Francis Joseph.

According to this communication, the German Emperor asked the Austrian Emperor to recognize Germany's annexation of Alsace and Lorraine, and to guarantee it 'against aggression'!

Bismarck has requested M. Thiers to appoint an ambassador to Berlin. M. Thiers offered the post to the Comte d'Harcourt, who refused, preferring to remain in Rome.

M. de Villemessant tells in the *Figaro* of visits to the Comte de Chambord at Lucerne and the Duc d'Aumale in Paris. Of the fusion the Duc d'Aumale said:

'That is entirely a question for my nephew the Comte de Paris. Whatever he does will be well done. I have no ambition but to remain a simple citizen, and if France is menaced again and is in need of me, I will fight for her as I fought in the army of the Loire.

21st November 1871. In the *salons* of the presidency at Versailles, conversation centres on the negotiations at Lucerne for an agreement between the Comte de Paris and the Comte de Chambord. People in close touch with M. Thiers appear to believe in the existence of such an accord.

In the *salon* of the Maréchale de MacMahon it is being said that the Comte de Chambord is very hopeful of a restoration of the monarchy, and that his advice is not to precipitate matters. He says that the crises both at home and abroad will convert his most bitter critics—even M. Thiers himself.

22nd November 1871. Mme de Saulcy, a former lady-in-waiting of the Empress Eugénie, who was to join her in England in the middle of this month, has postponed her departure because the empress will remain in Spain until the end of November. The French Government is closely watching the empress's movements to discover whether her presence in Spain is not connected with all the intrigues of the Bonapartists to prepare the return of Napoleon III.

25th November 1871. As the time approaches for the National Assembly to meet again, the Government is preparing the chamber of the Palais-Bourbon in Paris. Work was already started when the National Assembly first met in Bordeaux. The deputies will be rather cramped in this chamber, which was made for 400 people, and which must now hold 765! All sorts of expedients have been sought to increase the number of seats. Several deputies, notably M. de Walewski, went there yesterday to reserve their desks, but they discovered that the Government had issued an order that nobody, not even a deputy, was to be allowed inside the building until it was decided whether the National Assembly is to return to Paris.

Some eighty-five naval and military officers asked permission to visit the Comte de Chambord at Lucerne. The Government raised no objection as long as they travelled in civilian clothes, and in a strictly personal capacity.

The police have told M. Thiers that the slump on the Bourse is the work of three individuals in the pay of the Prussian Government. M. Thiers notified these people that they would be deported if they did not cease their operations.

29th November 1871. The Duc de la Rochefoucauld-Bisaccia, the Marquis de Mornay, and the Marquis de Rochejacquelin, and some other deputies, are back from Lucerne. These gentlemen have told me all about their visit to the Comte de Chambord. I have the honour to pass on to you this information. You will remember that the Marquis de Mornay went to Lucerne to communicate to the Comte de Chambord a proposition put forward by the Comte de Paris during his stay at the château of

Montchevreuil. The suggestion was that it should be left to the National Assembly to vote a Royalist constitution.

Here is the Comte de Chambord's answer:

'I am the king. I represent the only principle which can save France. My cousins recognize me as king, and I await their visit. I admit having come to Lucerne in the hope they would come to see me. My arms are wide open to receive them. If there have been any misunderstandings between us, now is the time to meet and discuss them frankly.

'My last manifesto clearly set out my policy. I can make no alteration to it. The days of compromise and false expedients are over, for these have proved fatal to France. I am unable to place myself without reserve in the hands of a National Assembly which is dominated by so many divergent influences, and which could introduce into the constitution fundamentals that are opposed to the principles I represent. I am much more in step with the times than many people realize, and I am prepared to admit to my cause all honest patriots, of whatever party they belong.'

A visitor suggested that France was grievously ill and ready to sample any cure that a charlatan brought along.

The Comte de Chambord interrupted him with these words:

'You are seeking a solution for the present crisis? But what solution, my dear sir? I am the solution.'

The Marquis de Mornay, unable to obtain any concrete answer to the Comte de Paris's suggestion, left Lucerne. A companion, the Marquis de Fourner, stayed beyind for a private talk with the Comte de Monti, Henri V's confidant. The idea was that the Comte de Monti could speak more freely than his royal master.

30th November 1871. The Marquis de Fourner's interview with the Comte de Monti took place on 24th November.

M. de Monti spoke with all the frankness that is characteristic of a Breton nobleman.

'The Orleanist princes have behaved very badly,' he said.

'Monseigneur has no concessions to make and will no longer suffer any intrigue. He told, in his manifesto, who he was and what he wanted. Nothing will make him change his mind. The Orleanist princes are too busy thinking of their own interests, instead of thinking only of their country.'

These are the last words from Lucerne.

Thus the Orleanist princes recognize the Comte de Chambord as King of France, but they refuse to make public their recognition of him until he has made an accord with the majority in the Chamber. The Comte de Chambord says: 'If you want a return to the hereditary monarchy, I am the king. All the princes of my family must give me their support. When the nation calls me it will find me ready to govern as liberally as is compatible with order.'

The visitors to the château say they found in Henri V the same calm, the same smiling serenity and unshaken confidence, as in Pope Pius IX. One of them added:

'The Comte de Chambord is a lay Pius IX.'

5th December 1871. The deputies are much preoccupied by the stubborn sympathy surviving in our rural districts and amongst the middle classes for Napoleon III. This is what some of them, back from their constituencies, were telling me at Versailles yesterday:

'The peasants and the workmen are sorry that the Second Empire has disappeared because under that regime they were so prosperous that they did not have to envy the rich. It is no good talking to them about the military disasters of Napoleon III because they answer that the emperor was betrayed by the wealthy classes. They excuse his capitulation at Sedan by saying that he did this to prevent shedding the blood of his soldiers uselessly.'

The departments of the Nord and of the Pas-de-Calais are almost exclusively Bonapartist. A deputy heard a woman shouting to a couple of peasants in the fields one day last week:

'Ah! If only we could have our good Napoleon III back again, what splendid times we should have.'

13th December 1871. Our deputies spend a lot of time discussing their return to Paris. The bad weather is a powerful argument in favour of returning to the Palais-Bourbon, for the cold and the snow make Versailles a miserable spot to live in.

M. Thiers and M. Casimir Périer are putting forward political, diplomatic, administrative, and financial reasons for leaving Versailles. Their opponents claim that a return to the capital would give too great a satisfaction to the Demagogy.

For the moment all is calm.

The debate on the amnesty will doubtless be heated because we shall be assailed by all the wives, daughters, and sisters of imprisoned leaders of the Commune.

The majority does not take M. Thiers's repeated threats to resign very seriously. They consider him a spoiled child, who has his moments of sulking. They add cynically that when he is worn out they will find somebody to replace him.

XI. THE FALL OF THIERS

2ND *January 1872.* While M. Thiers held his official New Year receptions at Versailles, the Duc d'Aumale received his friends and supporters at his home in the Faubourg Saint-Honoré. Many civil and military guests were there. The prince is giving a series of political dinners, and is playing a growing role in the affairs of the country. Princess Mathilde has not yet been able to take up residence at her house in the rue de Courcelles, and is staying with Princess Christine Bonaparte in the rue de Berry. Princess Mathilde is chiefly anxious to remain quietly in Paris, and to give M. Thiers no excuse to ask her to leave France. For this reason politics are never discussed in her *salon.* She has still a vast number of admirers.

11th January 1872. Though the Duc d'Aumale has not yet made his maiden speech he is doing everything he can to widen his sphere of influence. He takes infinite trouble to meet his colleagues, and to ask each his name, shaking hands with a multitude of people.

His receptions in Paris are increasingly attended by deputies, and amongst these are Legitimists like the youthful Marquis de Castellane, who is entirely deserting M. Thiers.

13th January 1872. Most deputies who live in Paris left for Versailles to-day because M. Thiers is to speak on the budget. Though the Chamber is tired of these frequent financial discussions, there is no choice but to raise the money to pay the war indemnity.

[It was in May 1872 that the National Assembly discussed the one important measure of the year—the Military Service Bill.

General Chanzy, of whom we have had glimpses during his command of the army of the Loire, and whose subsequent retreat is considered one of the most brilliant military operations in history, was elected to the National Assembly in February 1871.

Amongst the first to urge the dissolution of the National Guard, which he described as being nothing more than an army of disorder, he enthusiastically nursed through the bill for five years' conscription.

The National Assembly broached the subject at a time not altogether opportune. Part of the territory was still under German occupation; it was necessary to limit discussions because Europe was looking on and might misconstrue indiscretions in public debate.

M. de Marcère, himself a member of the National Assembly, describing this period in his *L'Assemblée Nationale de 1871*, said:

'Our military disasters had not only been a great humiliation for us; they caused a big surprise, and people searched for the reasons of our inferiority, so unexpected in the military sphere. We attributed them to the fatal influence of ideas which prevailed during the Second Empire, a slackening of moral discipline in all forms of society; a predominance of vulgar pleasures and of the money which secures such pleasures; a certain abasement of character; all causing demoralization and a general *laisser-aller* which had even permeated the army. . . . A passionate desire for virtue overcame us.'

Chief of all, the men of 1872 looked, with something like admiration, at the Prussian military machine. This sense of admiration may have hurt their pride, but they almost took satisfaction in doing penance.

The commission charged with elaborating a new military code was made up of the most distinguished men, most of whom had played important roles during the war. It sat under the presidency of the Marquis de Chasseloup-Laubat. Two main questions were discussed—the length of service, and compulsory service for everybody. The military reforms did not go through without considerable opposition. M. de Marcère said:

'Our race is essentially military and warlike, but it does not like unnecessary coercion. You will always find the Frenchman ready to fight if it is necessary, but he is slightly rebellious in barracks. It is to go against his instincts to force him . . . into compulsory military service.'

But it was imperative that the law should be passed. General Chanzy, in a remarkable speech, pleaded:

'Let us avoid long and burning discussions. Remember what happened in 1868 when Marshal Niel proposed a law to reform the army immediately after Sadowa. This law, which was so carefully prepared, was whittled down during public debate until nothing was left of it. And you know the result!

'We were beaten in 1870 because we had not enough men, and after our heroic little army fell gloriously at Wissembourg, at Frœschwiller, at Gravelotte, and at Sedan, there was nothing left in the rear but hastily improvised troops which, in spite of their patriotism, their perseverance, and their courage, could not mend the breach.']

14th November 1872. M. Thiers, by his message [to the National Assembly] yesterday, has severed the last link that attached the president to the Royalist parties. It is impossible to give an idea of the irritation caused in the Monarchist camps by the Republican declarations of M. Thiers. The die has been cast; the struggle is about to take place between the Republic and the monarchy. The different parties that go to make up the Right do not propose to ask for the re-establishment of the monarchy because they would not obtain a majority for such a motion, but they will protest against every attempt to constitute a Republic.

10th December 1872. A shipowner from Le Havre and two colleagues from Bordeaux called on M. Thiers to discuss the Communist propaganda in those seaports. The three men told M. Thiers that they have always voted for him, but that they could not continue to give him their political support unless his Government took a more active line against the Demagogy.

3rd January 1873. The deputies are much impressed by the many messages from their constituents stressing their desire for peace and a cessation of political quarrels. The public insists that both M. Thiers and the National Assembly should maintain the *status quo* or rapidly find a new constitution.

Workmen in Paris are divided in their opinion about choosing Citizen Ranc to replace M. Sauvage, former director of the

Eastern Railroad Company, in the Chamber. Many Parisians suspect that Ranc was an *agent provocateur* for M. Thiers during the Commune, and they would prefer to vote for a typical working man rather than for a professional agitator.

6th January 1873. The Bonapartists are much preoccupied by the illness of Napoleon III and the possible repercussions of his death. It is agreed that his disappearance would be a severe blow to the cause, but it would naturally be argued that his son, who will be of age in a few months, cannot be held responsible for his father's mistakes.

As the Comte de Chambord has no children, and as the Orleanist princes have lost much of their influence, the Bonapartists believe that if anything happened to Henri V they could rally many Monarchists to the Napoleonic dynasty.

M. Thiers, like Napoleon III, has a mania for discovering new military weapons—especially artillery. He has drawn the plans of a new gun that is to be tried out at Calais this week.

7th January 1873. During a meeting of the Army Council the Duc d'Aumale hazarded an opinion in which his political views were mixed up with his suggestions for the reorganization of the army.

M. Thiers snapped:

'Politics, in my experience, only mean one thing, the art of jockeying oneself into power, and then remaining in the saddle.'

In spite of the optimistic bulletins about the emperor's health in the Napoleonic newspapers, confidential dispatches from our ambassador in London suggest that the emperor will not survive the dangerous operations he must undergo.

Gambetta's newspaper, the *République Française*, appears to be amply supplied with funds. It has just moved to new premises with a rent of 26,000 francs a year. This paper is chiefly financed by M. Arnauld de l'Ariège, and it represents one man rather than a party.

Gambetta insisted that a private entrance, a private staircase, and a suite of private rooms should be built for him in the new building so that his visitors may come and see him secretly. Does this mean that there are many distinguished people who do not want it to be known that they frequent the company of Citizen Gambetta?

To those who continually blame M. Thiers for not breaking with the Left wing, our veteran statesman answers:

'Louis-Philippe and Napoleon III fell because they would have nothing to do with the Left.'

M. Thiers has hit on a queer scheme for our diplomatic representation in Rome. He wants to appoint a Catholic to the Vatican and a Protestant to the Quirinal.

'This,' he says, 'would be an excuse for our Protestant diplomat not to visit the Vatican.'

9th January 1873. A number of Conservative deputies have tabled the following motion:

'That this Assembly will not adjourn before the complete liberation of the territory and before establishing a Government which is in conformity with the permanent interests of the nation.'

The Paris police have, for some time, been on the lookout for one of the chief agents of the Internationale. This individual has just been arrested at Muret, near the Pyrenees, and is said to have made many important disclosures.

I was right to put you on guard against optimistic reports about Napoleon's health. His condition is desperate.

10th January 1873. Here are the different impressions I gather regarding the death of Napoleon III.

Complete indifference amongst most of the population; sincere regret amongst the small group which was personally attached to him; disappointment amongst the senators, deputies, and civil servants of the Second Empire, who still clung to the belief that the regime would be reinstated; despondency amongst the men who were plotting for his return.

Fear is now expressed that open warfare will take place between the empress and Prince Napoleon. You will recall that Prince Napoleon used to say with brutal cynicism during his cousin's reign:

'The only real Napoleonic blood is on my side.'

There are a few rash people in the party who still hope that the empress will attempt a landing with her son. The Empress Eugénie always admired the courage of the Duchesse de Berry, who, during the reign of Louis-Philippe, tried to foment a revolution in the Vendée in favour of her son, the Comte de Chambord.

M. Thiers does not hide his personal satisfaction at the news of Napoleon's death. The president believes that the Bonapartists will disintegrate now that their chief has disappeared.

13th January 1873. In spite of all the clamour in the Napoleonic newspapers over the grave of the emperor, the latest information from the provinces confirms what I told you about the complete indifference with which the news of his death has been received.

Even the peasants, who voted so enthusiastically for him in the last plebiscite, and who acclaimed him so frenziedly when he drove through their midst, remain unmoved.

It is true that this apathy is common to every political party.

The men who are actually in power are accepted without enthusiasm. That is what eighty years of revolutions have brought us to.

The Maréchale MacMahon, speaking of her husband, once said:

'As long as the emperor lives Maurice will never consider himself quite free.'

But not only has the marshal abstained from going to England to pay his last respects to the emperor, but he has publicly declared that his post as Commander-in-Chief of the Army forbids him to visit the empress.

It is now known that everything was planned for a landing by Napoleon III in March. Several generals on the coast were ready to acclaim him.

14th January 1873. The manifestations in favour of Napoleon IV have greatly angered M. Thiers, who has asked the Minister of Justice if the Napoleonic newspapers cannot be prosecuted. The owners of these papers are determined, however, to carry on.

Bonapartists left for Chislehurst very hostile towards Prince Napoleon. They will advise the empress to break off relations with him, because otherwise her son's chances will, they say, be ruined.

The emperor had prepared plans for the Government he intended to set up in March. France was to be divided into seventeen provinces, each with its university. Free education was to be provided for every child.

27th January 1873. My brother, who has a villa at Cannes, had a long talk yesterday with M. Estancelin, who is on intimate terms with the Orleanist princes. M. Estancelin said:

'For a long time I have entreated the princes to translate their words into action, and to visit Henri V at Frohsdorf, but the princes are so incapable of making up their minds that their indecision amounts to a disease. The Duc d'Aumale is the most irresolute of them all.'

28th January 1873. The Committee of Thirty, appointed to draw up the outline of general policy, has been discussing the formation of a second Chamber. M. de Larcy left the committee room beaming with pleasure, in spite of the fatigue of a twelve hours' session, for it was decided that in future when M. Thiers wishes to address the National Assembly he will be obliged to send a message to that effect. The debate will be adjourned, and the president heard on the following day. The debate will not be resumed until the president has left the Chamber.

M. Thiers's scheme for a second Chamber will fail.

To the delight of the Conservatives the members of the Left voted against it, and the announcement that the question will

Henri V, Comte de Chambord

be raised at some future date is meant merely to soften the blow for the president.

Long conferences took place all night between M. Thiers and the Left. It is clear that the situation is critical, and that the Conservative majority is on the eve of seizing power.

29th January 1873. M. Thiers's anger with the Committee of Thirty is such that if he is called to address it he may easily lose his self-control. The deputies are expecting a long and lively debate in the Chamber to-morrow, when the Assembly will be called upon to dismiss the Communist municipal council and mayor of Lyons.

A number of prefects in the Rhône are accused of preventing sentences of imprisonment being passed by the judges on leaders of the Commune.

8th March 1873. After M. Thiers had addressed the National Assembly, Citizen Gambetta, passing through the corridor of the Chamber, remarked to a fellow deputy:

'How Thiers has changed! He has just made the speech of a centenarian. I don't give him three months.'

I had a long talk yesterday with M. Pouyer-Quertier, who, more than anybody, seconded M. Thiers in his financial policy.

'This debate is enough to make one despair,' he sighed. 'We see the Monarchists voting for a law that will lay the foundations of the Republic, and the Republicans voting against their own interests.'

M. Thiers is said to have had an attack of apoplexy. He has certainly undergone a terrible change during the last few days.

17th March 1873. Sixty deputies of the Left, none from the Right, called on M. Thiers yesterday to congratulate him on his successful negotiations for the liberation of our territory.

The final milliard of the indemnity is to be paid in four equal instalments between now and 5th September. The whole of France, except Verdun, is to be liberated on 30th July, long before the date originally fixed. Verdun itself will be evacuated on 15th September.

The National Assembly does not intend to wind up for some time after the actual evacuation. I have heard the view expressed that the final session will be held from September of this year until May of next year.

Many deputies want to appoint a vice-president of the Republic before they go off for the Easter recess, fearing that something might happen to M. Thiers during their absence, but the president will not hear of it. As his influence has greatly increased since his success in liberating our territory, he will certainly get his own way.

Foreigners are flocking to Paris. The hotels and apartment houses are packed. Friends of mine who wanted to find a flat in the Champs-Élysées for a two months' stay have been unable to obtain anything.

7th May 1873. The president is rapidly losing ground again, even amongst those who until recently were his closest supporters. He counted chiefly on the financial world, and it is from that quarter that he is most bitterly attacked. He seems to be at the end of his political expedients.

14th May 1873. Discussions are taking place between the Conservative deputies about the possible repercussions of M. Thiers's resignation if that should take place. Many members of the majority are in favour of appointing Marshal MacMahon to replace him because of the marshal's influence over the army, though it is admitted that politically he is a weak man.

20th May 1873. The Conservative majority has been warned that unless it can force M. Thiers to resign this week he will have time to gain enough support to remain in power. An adjournment of the debate would allow the president to negotiate, rally the waverers, and become once again master of the situation.

[Towards the end of the session of 23rd May a member of the Cabinet announced that M. Thiers wished to address the National Assembly. It was decided to hear him the following day, 24th May.

The president mounted the tribune at the beginning of the debate. Never did he rise to greater heights of eloquence. A crowded and expectant house had the impression that he was engaged in a duel with his adversary, the Duc de Broglie, champion of those Conservatives who were determined to deal a death-blow to the Republic in the person of its president.

M. de Broglie had resigned from the post of ambassador in London to lead the battle against M. Thiers. A grandson of the writer Mme de Staël, he was a man of great culture and nicety of manners, but his timidity gave him a supercilious air, and he did not hide his contempt for democracy, which he considered vulgar.

M. Thiers's emotion was plain for all to see. He spoke with marked dignity and a knowledge of the great cause he represented.

He was overthrown; but, thanks to him, France had already risen.

The Monarchists sacrificed this great patriot because he had proclaimed his undying allegiance to the Republic. Their action might have been justified if they had immediately proclaimed a monarchy, but they did nothing more than replace one president of the Republic with another, one set of ministers with another set.

Ironically, they themselves were to lay the foundations for the future Republican constitution. Marshal MacMahon was immediately elected successor to M. Thiers, but with this difference, that whereas M. Thiers had governed from the tribune almost like a dictator, the soldier-president was to hold a watching brief from without the Chamber in accordance with the maxim: 'The president presides but does not govern.'

While the marshal was instructing M. de Broglie to form a Cabinet, M. Thiers's associates visited him at home. It was close on midnight. They found him exhausted, asleep in an arm-chair by the dying embers of a coal fire. The ministers, sad and discouraged, took their places round a table, and waited for their chief to wake. After a time he opened his eyes, rose, and shook each by the hand, thanking them for coming.]

opportunity of seeing their new army. We were all impressed by these splendid troops.

The shopkeepers pictured a shah loaded with diamonds and precious stones, and buying everything that took his fancy. Alas, the shah's Chancellor of the Exchequer warned him that he must be careful with his money, because in Berlin he bought 110,000 French Chassepot rifles which the Germans sold him cheap!

The Republic is being kept in the background during the present rejoicings, and foreign visitors are particularly surprised because they imagined all Parisians to be enthusiastic Republicans.

23rd July 1873. The Government has asked newspaper editors not to print too many anti-German articles until our territory has been entirely liberated. Dr Tholozen, the shah's doctor, says he was shocked by the intense German hatred of everything French.

24th July 1873. My house in the rue du Bel Respiro was struck by lightning last night. A chimney was thrown against the balcony of my terrace; a gas pipe in my apartment caught alight and nearly set fire to the whole house. There is a great deal of talk at the Bourse about the financial troubles of the Duc de Broglie, and the negotiations carried out by his agents, who are trying to raise a loan of 2,000,000 francs for him. They seem to be meeting with great difficulty. People are wondering what is the reason for such financial embarrassment.

5th August 1873. Another proof of how little the country is Republican at heart is the huge interest in the departure of the Comte de Paris for Vienna, and his coming visit to the head of the house of Bourbon. This is the subject of every conversation in every class of society. The Comte de Paris seeks to re-establish the unity of the house of Bourbon, which has been divided since Louis-Philippe's accession in 1830.

Before leaving for Vienna the Comte de Paris took his wife and children to Villers-sur-Mer (Calvados).

M. Édouard Hervé arrived at the villa that evening, and in the presence of the Comte de Paris wrote the article published in Paris on 3rd August, in which the Comte de Chambord is loyally recognized as the sole representative of hereditary monarchy.

This article, which meets with the entire approval of the Conservative majority, more than ever desirous of deciding the country's constitution before the end of the year, clearly sets out the motives of the Comte de Paris's visit to Frohsdorf.

The followers of M. Thiers, the Republicans, and the Bonapartists are hoping against hope that some miracle will prevent this reunion, but the Conservatives are determined to achieve it at all costs.

8th August 1873. It would be almost worth while betting that a monarchy will be re-established in a single night. In addition to the Extreme Right, the Right, and the Centre Right, there are eighty to one hundred Conservative members without any particular feelings about a dynasty, who, in the face of events, would be disposed to vote for the monarchy, giving a majority of 250 votes in the National Assembly.

The king will be warned, and will go to Versailles. The next morning Parisians will wake up to find a royal proclamation, and His Majesty will make a triumphal entry into Paris to numerous cries of: 'Vive le Roi!' There will be many white flags hanging from the windows.

That is what is being prepared.

I sometimes talk to the foreman of 'Denière,' which is near my office in the rue Vivienne.

This man, whose home is at Montrouge, told me yesterday that all the small shopkeepers in his district are hoping for the arrival of Henri V, not from any particular feelings for the dynasty, but simply because they want the security which they feel a monarchy represents.

6th September 1873. The coming liberation of our territory, the calm which reigns all over France, and the hope of a constitution to confirm the country's stability, continue to inspire confidence on the Bourse, where prices continue to rise.

23rd September 1873. There is a very firm tendency on the Bourse. Large blocks of shares are changing hands, reflecting general confidence in the situation.

30th September 1873. The decrees in the *Journal Officiel* re-organizing the army have made a splendid impression. The fact that they are published so soon after the last of the Germans have left our territory proves that we intend to create a strong army able to meet any emergency.

20th October 1873. Everybody in Paris and the provinces is prepared for a monarchy. Parisians view the return of a king calmly—almost with indifference—as if it was the normal thing to happen.

Prince Napoleon went to see M. Thiers to-day, telling him that, although he detested his politics, he would gladly place himself at his disposal to prevent the return of the Bourbons.

28th October 1873. Gambetta and Challemel-Lacour are still hopeful of saving the Republic.

They point out that there are twenty-five deputies who have not yet made up their minds. The Radicals are holding mass meetings all over France. There are rumours that they plan to kidnap the Marquise de MacMahon, the marshal's niece, and keep her as a hostage.

29th October 1873. Marshal MacMahon told the generals who are to take up their new commands that the monarchy was about to be re-established and that they must shape their conduct with this in mind.

'The Government and the Conservative majority cannot fail on this issue,' he said. 'At the worst I am prepared to throw in the weight of my personal authority.'

31st October 1873. A deputy of the Right this morning compared the Comte de Chambord's letter [of 27th October] to a blow from an oar on a drowning man who thought he was within reach of the rescue boat.

All the delicate negotiations of the last three months between the princes and the various groups of the parliamentary majority are wrecked just as victory seemed in sight.

What can be done now?

Appoint the Comte de Paris lieutenant-general?

Prolong Marshal MacMahon's mandate either indefinitely or for a fixed number of years?

Proclaim the Republic as a permanent regime?

Whilst despair and confusion sweep the Conservative ranks, M. Thiers, the Bonapartists, and the Republicans are in the seventh heaven of delight. The Comte de Chambord's letter produced a slump at the Bourse, which would have proved even more serious had not the Government stepped in to absorb the heavy liquidation.

3rd November 1873. Marshal MacMahon has become master of the situation, and the Conservative majority will be obliged to do everything he wishes. Thus we have returned more than ever to a personal Government.

Under a cloak of modesty and indifference, the marshal has acquired a taste for power and a desire not only to keep his authority, but to extend it. The Conservatives called on him to-day to place themselves obediently at his disposal. He has even his flatterers, like the Duc d'Audiffret-Pasquier, who urged the Committee of Nine to vote the president-marshal a life mandate in a speech that was a real deluge of verbose admiration.

The Duc de la Rochefoucauld-Bisaccia called out:

'But you 're offering us a king *à la polonaise*!'

27th December 1873. The Orleanist princes do not cease deploring the Comte de Chambord's letter, which has destroyed all hope of a monarchy.

The Duc de Nemours said to-day:

'How sad that our cousin does not understand public opinion better. He is willing to accept everybody's dictatorship except his own. Did not the deep affection shown by Frenchmen to the tricolour during Marshal Bazaine's trial for treason prove how impossible it is to ask the nation to abandon its flag?'

The Duc d'Aumale, president of the Bazaine court martial, attended a banquet last night. A learned judge brought thirteen bottles of the most delicious wine from his own vineyard, and during a little speech said:

'When King Henri IV entered Poligny in 1595 he asked for a glass of local wine. Having drunk it he declared it excellent, and there was no better judge than he.

'"Ah! We've got even better than that!" boasted a wine grower.

'King Henri IV laughed. "I suppose," he said, "that you are keeping it for a more appropriate occasion?"'

The judge, having told this story, added:

'I brought these bottles from my vineyard because I have none better to offer the Duc d'Aumale, worthy descendant of Henri IV.'

3rd January 1874. The Duc d'Aumale has just returned from an inspection of his military command at Besançon.

I do not need to stress the strategic importance of this city.

The Duc d'Aumale's personal friends say that he was extremely dissatisfied by the defence of this portion of our eastern frontier. He wrote a long letter to the military commission giving details of the inadequacy of material and troops. The Minister of War complained bitterly to Marshal MacMahon that the Duc d'Aumale addressed his remarks to the military commission rather than to him.

M. Thiers has become more economical than ever.

One of my friends who dined with him in Paris a couple of nights ago tells me that the dinner was even worse than when M. Thiers entertained at Versailles during his presidency.

The conversation turned on M. de Bismarck's persecution of

the Catholic Church. Edmond de Pressensé, the noted Protestant pastor, severely blamed Bismarck for his savage attacks on the priests.

M. Thiers exclaimed:

'I have always said to every Government: "Never touch the Catholic Church!"'

8th January 1874. Marshal MacMahon and the army have no anxiety about the situation at home, but they are extremely worried about the attitude of the Cabinets of Berlin and Rome.

They are convinced that these two powers are about to declare war on us.

One of our ministers exclaimed to-day:

'What a terrible responsibility we have, for we are not ready.'

A letter from Berlin discloses that by next month the German army will be increased by at least 225,000 men, making a total of 1,500,000. The German papers have started a campaign, on the orders of Berlin, accusing France of building up immense armaments to attack Germany!

15th January 1874. Since the National Assembly prolonged Marshal MacMahon's term of office to seven years, preventing him from being overthrown by an adverse vote in the Assembly, there have been conflicting interpretations of his powers.

Does the prolongation imply that no attempt may henceforth be made to bring back the monarchy? The Conservatives are asking themselves this question. Meanwhile they intend to vote such laws as may be to their ultimate advantage.

20th January 1874. The marshal-president is alarmed about Prussia's preparations to wage war on us. It is said that we may be attacked in the spring.

31st March 1874. In the Bonapartist *salons* Marshal MacMahon is being called Mac-bête (Macbeth).

4th April 1874. M. Louis Veuillot, in an article in *L'Univers*, says:

'For the last fifty years M. Thiers has been the phylloxera of politics.'

28th April 1874. Calm reigns amongst Frenchmen.

Confidence is returning not only in Paris but in the provinces. If this continues, and if the Government retains its majority, there is every reason to suppose that we shall witness a strong business recovery, for there are vast sums of idle money waiting for investment.

9th May 1874. The deputies have found the nation so eager for calm, rest, and stability that they have returned to work determined to avoid all causes of conflict, and anxious to consolidate the marshal's authority.

21st May 1874. The Princesse de Metternich is very bitter against the Comte Jean de Montebello.

This quarrel dates from the war of 1870.

When news of Sedan and the capture of Napoleon III was brought to the club, where the count was playing cards, he turned to his friends and exclaimed:

'Ah! The emperor is a prisoner. Then, gentlemen, I play the king!'

2nd June 1874. England, Russia, and Austria are determined to prevent Prussia from attacking France a second time without a serious motive.

Lord Derby's energetic action three months ago was chiefly responsible for preventing Bismarck from declaring war on us. England, Russia, and Austria have let it be known in Berlin that they will side with us against any aggressor.[1]

5th June 1874. During a reception given by Marshal Mac-Mahon at Versailles last evening, the leaders of the various groups of the National Assembly showed some anxiety about the lack of political unity.

Several generals crowded round one of our principal Cabinet ministers, and said to him:

'The Government must do something; otherwise the Empire will come back.'

---

[1] England alone intervened unmistakably. Russian influence was in the same direction, but Austria was much too close to Germany by now.

Though this Cabinet minister is a man of resource, he found nothing better to answer than:

'But what can we do?'

This is typical of our Government.

The Cabinet is still anxiously waiting to see what Bismarck will do. M. de Gontant-Biron, our ambassador to Germany, urges the Government to do nothing to offend Berlin. Meanwhile the German Cabinet is trying to intimidate the Spanish Government into making an alliance with Germany and Italy against France.

10th June 1874. A deputy said to me yesterday:

'Marshal MacMahon is an honest man without intellect. M. Thiers is a man of intellect without honesty.'

25th June 1874. Why do all the cab drivers read the *Rappel*?

I discovered this yesterday while being driven to the Bois de Boulogne by a loquacious cabby.

He was complaining about the lack of a real Government and the instability of things in general, and added that the best thing would be to return to the Empire.

'But if you and your colleagues are Bonapartists,' I put in, 'why do you read the Socialist *Rappel*?'

He answered:

'Each time that a cab driver has an accident or gets mixed up in a quarrel with a fare, the *Figaro*, the *Gaulois*, and the other papers attack him. But the *Rappel* always takes his side. That is why we buy it.'

8th July 1874. M. Thiers is very busy.

As you know, he has never forgiven Marshal MacMahon for taking his place. He said to me yesterday:

'The marshal has stolen everything from me—even my hatred for the Legitimists.'

11th August 1874. M. Napoléon Bonaparte Wise has revealed that Victor Emmanuel's chief minister, M. Minighetti, is in the pay of Prussia, and that he is at present at Kissingen with Prince Bismarck.

19th August 1874. The Breton peasants call Marshal Mac-Mahon 'the King of the Republic.'

During his journey through Brittany the marshal passed through Morlaix, where many workmen followed his carriage shouting: 'Long live the Republic!' and singing the *Marseillaise.* Others carried Chinese lanterns, and cried: 'Liberté, Égalité, Fraternité—ou la mort!'

3rd October 1874. M. Thiers has turned himself into the Republic's commercial traveller. He journeys far and wide announcing that the Republic will soon become France's permanent regime. The members of the Cabinet are furious about this crusade, and they show each other translations from the Italian newspapers that describe M. Thiers's recent conversations with King Victor Emmanuel at Turin.

As M. Thiers is not always a model of discretion it is quite possible that he gave Italian reporters an account of his talk with Victor Emmanuel. At any rate, the papers claim that he said that the Republic would be proclaimed officially in France next winter, and that even the Royalists would help to found it.

Shares on the Bourse were very weak on account of this.

19th October 1874. The tendency of the elections is increasingly Republican and gives the members of the Cabinet occasion for much anxious thought. It appears certain that the parliamentary majority will soon become Radical.

Strong buying has made shares rise on the Bourse. Messages have arrived from all over France telling of the arrival of foreign buyers, who are placing orders for immense quantities of wine, wheat, and fruit. They are spending money lavishly.

24th October 1874. Marshal MacMahon and his Cabinet are becoming less nervous about Prussia's intentions towards us. Great Britain and Russia are responsible for this. Though the Prince of Wales's visit to Paris has officially nothing to do with politics, it has immensely contributed to better relations between our two countries. His influence is very favourable to us.

The Duc de la Rochefoucauld-Bisaccia, during the shoot at Rambouillet yesterday, said to me:

'Nobody realizes how much we owe to the Prince of Wales.'

There is a tremendous wave of confidence on the Bourse.

27th October 1874. A German diplomat tells me that great enmity continues towards France all over north Germany and the Prussians are boasting that they will smash us as soon as they get a chance.

At the court in Berlin people stress the unbridled arrogance of M. de Bismarck, and his impatience, which suffers no contradiction even from the emperor.

11th November 1874. The breach between Marshal Mac-Mahon and the Comte de Chambord is now wider than ever.

This separation dates from the day that the marshal refused to meet the head of the house of Bourbon at Versailles on 10th November last year.

The Comte Stanislas de Blacas, a relative by marriage of the MacMahon family, went to see the *maréchale*, to tell her that the Comte de Chambord was in Paris, and anxious to see her husband.

The *maréchale* answered that her husband was at that moment in conference with the Duc de Broglie, and offered to give the Comte de Blacas an answer the next day.

This delay gave the marshal an opportunity to consult the leaders of the Centre Right. When the Comte de Blacas returned the following morning he met with a refusal.

M. de Blacas wrote an angry letter to the marshal complaining of the way he had treated the Comte de Chambord, but it was chiefly against the *maréchale* that the prince and his followers showed their bitterness, for they knew how great was her influence over the marshal.

16th December 1874. At Versailles people are repeating a witty remark by General Changarnier, who turned to the deputies sitting beside him as he voted for the new law to protect children, and whispered:

'This Assembly is so incapable of giving birth to anything that it is quite right to look after other people's children!'

One of my daughters attended a ball last evening at Joigny.

The bassoon player in the orchestra had just been elected a Radical member of the municipal council!

Frohsdorf Castle, in Austria, where the Duc de Chambord spent his exile until 1870

Charles X leaving for Exile in England, 1830
With Charles X are his daughter-in-law, the Duchesse de Berry, and her ten-year-old son, the future Comte de Chambord

XIII. THE REPUBLIC CONFIRMED

26TH *January 1875*. The fate of the constitutional laws will be decided this week.

Before discussing the creation of the Senate the National Assembly will debate the draft of the measure proposed by M. de Ventavon, chairman of the Committee of Thirty. The battle for the Republic will be fought on this bill.

The public is so anxious for a solution to be reached that it believes any rumour. Six generals are said to have told Marshal MacMahon that they will put their army corps at his disposal if the National Assembly refuses to vote the constitution. The marshal himself has threatened to hold a plebiscite.

The Bourse is so firm that people say that the Rente will touch 105 before long.

4th February 1875. The National Assembly is anxious for a few days' reflection before deliberating the constitutional laws for the third time. The vote to create the Senate is to take place first.

The Wallon amendment which was passed on 30th January by 353 votes to 352 has, however, already proclaimed the Republic as the future regime of France.

This was the text:

'The President of the Republic is elected by the absolute majority of votes of the Senate and the Chamber of Deputies united in a National Assembly. He is appointed for a term of seven years. He is re-eligible.'

Marshal MacMahon, on learning last evening of the suppression of his title of Marshal in that of President of the Republic, became extremely angry—so angry that the *maréchale* had difficulty to calm him.[1] This will not prevent him from

[1] C. de B. does not, of course, mean that Marshal MacMahon was deprived of his title of marshal. But whereas he had previously exerted an overwhelming authority by his personal prestige, he was obliged, by the constitution of 1875, to sink his individuality in the role of President of the

remaining in power in the conditions laid down by the constitutional laws.

At Versailles last evening it was claimed that a majority is assured for an additional clause that several deputies intend to propose, and which would forbid any prince of a royal or imperial family of France from holding the post of President of the Republic. The measure is chiefly directed against the Duc d'Aumale.

5th February 1875. Marshal MacMahon's reception at the Élysée last evening provided this interesting sidelight.

A large number of deputies of the Right and the Extreme Right decided to attend in order to tell the President of the Republic that he could rely on the support of their parties, which have hitherto figured in the Conservative majority.

I heard a good story about M. de Ventavon.

After the vote on the Wallon amendment, M. de Ventavon went up to M. Cazenave de Pradines and said to him:

'Imagine how embarrassed I am. I intended to make a seven years' presidency for the marshal, and I'm given a Republic!'

M. Cazenave answered:

'You're a white man, your wife is a white woman. She has given birth to a mulatto; you've only one thing to do—disown it.'

And so he has. M. de Ventavon has resigned from the Committee of Thirty!

8th February 1875. During the holidays of the carnival the leading members of the Centre Left, the Left, and the dissidents of the Centre Right are meeting to organize the Senate.

M. Thiers is using all his diplomacy and persuasiveness to achieve this crowning triumph of the Republic.

There are even a few members of the Moderate Right, like

Republic. Not the marshal, but the President of the Republic, was now nominated for seven years. Paul Deschanel (in *Gambetta*, Paris, 1919) wrote: 'His powers [those of the President of the Republic] no longer emanating from the direct suffrage of the whole nation, nobody will any longer consider the guardian of the law as superior to the representatives of the country who make the law.' Jacques Bainville wrote: 'The Republic lost its worst defects by the transition of the "maréchalat."'

the Comte de Rességuier, who intend to go over to the Republican majority.

The Comte de Rességuier said to me yesterday:

'If I cannot make a monarchy I will vote for the Republic, rather than allow the Empire to come back.'

Let me tell you something about the new opera house.

Subscribers say that the boxes are too small. M. Charles Garnier, the architect of this masterpiece, which has taken twelve years to build, will not hear of carpets being laid down in the vestibule because they would hide his mosaics. The result is that the long dresses of the women sweep the floor!

The hall where subscribers wait for their carriages is much too small. There was a magnificent staircase in the old opera house, where everybody used to gather. It was a fine sight after the performance. In addition to this there was the big room overlooking the rue Lepelletier.

11th February 1875. The deputies of the Left do not hide their intention of overthrowing Marshal MacMahon. They say:

'We've got the old dummy where we want him. He won't cramp our style much longer.'[1]

18th February 1875. Confidence and strength continue on the Bourse, which no longer takes any notice of what is happening at Versailles. It's wonderful to see the way dividends are being resumed.

The Rente has passed 102.

19th February 1875. The marshal's sudden resolve, on the advice of his ministers, to support the Wallon measure for the organization of the Senate, has produced a tremendous impression.

It means a complete break with the Right, and the formation of a new parliamentary majority.

M. Thiers exclaimed in triumph:

'I shall soon have my revenge for 24th May.'

[That was the date in 1873 when Thiers was overthrown by the Right.]

[1] Nous le tenons maintenant ce mannequin. Il ne nous gênera guère plus longtemps.

The extraordinary rise with which the Bourse has welcomed the agreement reached between the marshal and the Right shows how impatient is public opinion to see the formation of a Government.

The Rente is now expected to touch 104 before the end of the month.

20th February 1875. I learn that the marshal is much saddened by the reproaches of his family and his old friends for turning his coat.

His niece, the Marquise de MacMahon, said to him:

'Marshal, you have dishonoured the name of our children by forming the Republic!'

The marshal answered:

'How can I persuade the nation to settle its differences when I cannot even obtain agreement amongst the members of my own family?'

22nd February 1875. We are nearing the formation of the Third Republic.

The parties of the Right are in confusion and despondency.

They are furious with the marshal, who, like Thiers, was put into power by the Monarchists only to sell out to the Republicans.

The *maréchale's* intimate friends speak of her preoccupation, her anxiety, and her sadness. On several occasions they have found her in tears. She constantly alludes to the days when she was so happy, and only speaks of the present with bitterness.

Deputies quote these words of Admiral Saisset:

'Marshal MacMahon is preparing for himself the fate of Louis XVI, with all the misfortunes of that monarch, less his grandeur.'

24th February 1875. The vote of the Wallon constitution puts us back to 1830.

The Orleanists are responsible for this parliamentary revolution. M. Wallon himself is a well-known Orleanist.

The fact that the Prince de Joinville voted for this bill shows that he obeyed the advice of the Comte de Paris. Thus the agreement reached with Henri V at Frohsdorf is broken, and there is once more bitter antagonism between the two Monarchist groups.

25th February 1875. Members who voted for the creation of the Senate are anxious that it should meet as soon as possible at the Luxembourg Palace in Paris, which would set a precedent for the return of the Chamber to the Palais-Bourbon.

The Bourse is becoming acclimatized to the idea of a Republic.

16th March 1875. A member of the Paris Municipal Council told me yesterday that his colleague, the celebrated coach-builder M. B., was now producing a carriage every day, and that his profit was 1,000 francs.

You will see that this represents a pretty sum at the end of a year.

12th April 1875. The people of Belfort are convinced that if it had not been for M. Thiers that city would have been annexed by the Germans. They have therefore a great affection for the former president. His portrait occupies a place of honour in every house.

There is a suggestion that M. Thiers should be elected to the Senate, but he has not yet decided whether to remain a deputy or not.

17th April 1875. Our Minister of Foreign Affairs goes in fear of receiving a new note from Prussia.

He says that the fierce propaganda in the German press about our alleged rearmament is simply a prelude to a demand for the complete disarmament of France.

As, in fact, we are not arming, and our military machine is on a strict peace footing, and far from complete at that, we should be obliged to refuse to take any action.

Is that the pretext which M. de Bismarck is waiting for to declare war?

21st April 1875. All the telegrams reaching the Ministry of Foreign Affairs from all our embassies at the principal courts of Europe tell of a general desire to maintain peace and to oppose every provocation of the Berlin Cabinet. Our military attachés in Prussia describe how Germany is feverishly fortifying her frontier.

29th April 1875. The Paris correspondent of the Bavarian *Gazette d'Augsbourg* is back from a ten days' tour in Germany. He claims that everybody in Germany is longing to attack us again. There is considerable distress on the other side of the Rhine, the scarcity of money is becoming more acute, and the tremendous war programme is taxing people beyond their endurance.

Prussians consider France as their prey whose spoils are necessary to alleviate their own misery. They say we have not paid enough, and they threaten to double our ransom next time.

2nd June 1875. M. Buffet tells a lot of stories about his journey with the marshal in the south of France.

To show how deeply the idea of monarchy is embedded in the minds of our peasants, he describes how the inhabitants of a small village, recognizing Marshal MacMahon, cried out:

'Long live His Majesty the President of the Republic!'

18th June 1875. The tranquillity at home and abroad is reflected in the strength of the Bourse.

21st June 1875. The Comtesse Walewska has arrived from Florence to prepare for the marriage of her second daughter to an official of the Council of State.

As this wealthy young man is said to be an Orleanist, the Bonapartists are extremely vexed by the marriage, and they say of the Comtesse Walewska:

'She has gone over to the enemy.'

It is being said at Versailles that Marshal MacMahon, wearied by the petty intrigues by which his enemies try to hinder his work, by the spiders' webs woven round him, and by all the string-pulling which to-day is inseparable with politics, exclaimed in a moment of anger at the Élysée:

'Do all these people think that I can direct the affairs of the nation as M. Thiers runs his mansion in the Place Saint-Georges?'

24th June 1875. Paris is in the middle of a building boom, such as we have not seen since the war.

25th June 1875. The Radicals are very angry with M. Gambetta for his speech a couple of nights ago at the Hoche banquet. They accuse the Republican lawyer from Genoa of going over to the *bourgeoisie*, and one of his bitterest critics exclaimed as he left the banquet:

'Gambetta has become Marshal MacMahon's Émile Ollivier!'

[Émile Ollivier was Napoleon III's chief minister.]

8th July 1875. The growing friendship between General de Cissey, War Minister, and M. Thiers, is much commented upon. M. de Cissey never fails to seek M. Thiers's advice on any important matter. A few days ago fears of German aggression were renewed, but have now calmed down. Nevertheless the War Minister is working hard to prepare our forces to withstand the first clash should hostilities break out.

11th July 1875. Financial circles are impressed by the great abundance of money, most of which is finding its way into the Rente.

22nd July 1875. The Radicals are very angry because Marshal MacMahon has given orders for the Republican emblem, 'Liberté, Egalité, Fraternité,' to be removed from the façade of the palace of the Élysée.

24th July 1875. The barometer, which has risen after several weeks heavy rain, is partly responsible for the rise on the Bourse; the political barometer, also at 'Set Fair,' has given a fillip to speculation.

2nd August 1875. There is no stopping the rise on the Bourse.

12th August 1875. It is necessary for me to point out how people everywhere in France are getting down to business and forgetting party politics. This is one of the results of our military disaster. Families are anxious to repair the ruin of their homes while the nation is rebuilding its vitality. Even the Radicals are unable to stir up trouble.

11th October 1875. The War Minister is shooting in the forest of Loches with the Comte Brainck. General de Cissey likes to talk with all those who come to see him. In this he is very different from Marshal MacMahon, who confines himself to a few monosyllables.

During the recent shoot at Rambouillet, to which many generals, prefects, and civil servants were invited, all eager to discuss their problems with the marshal, he never said more than:

'What a lovely day.'

'I wonder if we shall have a good bag?'

'Do you think the weather will be fine to-morrow?'

18th October 1875. French officers who were present at the German army manœuvres are now back, and have handed in their reports to the Ministry of War.

All of them are of the opinion that no nation has ever achieved so great a development of military power as Germany. They consider that the Germans can rush 300,000 men to Metz and Strasburg within three days. These two strongholds will prove the pivot of any future operations against France.

Germany is in a position to draft 700,000 to 800,000 men to our frontier in seven days, whereas in 1870 she took fifteen days to send 500,000 across the Rhine.

The Prussian officers treated our military attachés with that politeness and assiduous attention which they so often affect to mask their odious cruelty. In this case our compatriots found their attitude particularly humiliating.

Prince Frederick Charles was the only one honest enough to show his real feelings. He never spoke a word to our officers when they were introduced to him, but immediately turned his back.

On the other hand the German Emperor, after the big review, complimented our officers for coming, but added these ironical words:

'Criticism is easy, but the art of war is difficult.'

Commander Groley, who happened to be standing nearest the emperor, answered:

'Sire, our only reason for coming here is to learn.'

21st October 1875. Princess Lise Troubetzkoy, who entertained so brilliantly during the Second Empire, is back in Paris from Baden, and has reopened her *salon*, where she is anxious to gather distinguished leaders of every political party.

For the moment it is frequented especially by the followers of M. Thiers, by the Bonapartists, and by the Republicans.

One day, after Marshal Bazaine and the Duc d'Aumale had called on her, a well-known Legitimist arrived.

'What a pity you did not come earlier,' she exclaimed. 'You would have met Marshal Bazaine and the Duc d'Aumale.'

This craze for confronting such bitter political enemies once led her to invite M. Raoul Duval and M. Thiers to her *salon* at Ouchy one afternoon when both these men happened to be in Switzerland. M. Duval heard what was in store for him, and refused the invitation. I need hardly explain that M. Raoul Duval is a confirmed Bonapartist.

Diplomats call this princess the 'Great Question Mark.'

She is always asking the most awkward questions with the most unruffled air.

'Do you think that the Bonapartists will re-establish the Empire?'

'Do you suppose the Orleanists will succeed?'

'Will the Duc d'Aumale become president of the Senate?'

When M. Thiers was President of the Republic he gave her the right to send him free telegrams, and she made constant use of this privilege.

During the crisis that proved M. Thiers's downfall she wired to him:

'You are in danger. Join the princes and make an agreement with the dukes.'

M. Thiers wired back:

'Princes have no gratitude, and one can never trust dukes.'

16th November 1875. As the moment approaches for the National Assembly to be dissolved, the various Conservative groups realize the importance of drawing closer together.

The curious thing is that now we are in a Republic the Conservative majority which created it no longer exists.

Marshal Canrobert, who covered himself with glory during the defence of Saint-Privat in August 1870, was discussing politics with Marshal MacMahon at Versailles the other day.

The marshal said to him:

'Keep quiet, my good fellow. You're a brave soldier, but you don't know the first thing about politics!'

22nd November 1875. M. Dufaure outlined the following programme at Versailles yesterday:

The seventy-five life senators will be elected by the Assembly during the first days of December.

The municipal council will elect the senatorial delegates on 23rd or 24th December.

The provincial senators will be elected early in January.

The Chamber of Deputies will be elected at the end of January.

The Conservatives, whose chief support comes from the peasants, claim that they will be penalized by winter elections. There are many farms and villages miles away from the nearest polling booths and if there is snow many peasants will not trouble to vote.

20th December 1875. The deputies are getting ready for the dissolution.

Alas, many of them will not come back.

Those who have no chance of being elected to the Chamber of Deputies intend to go to the provinces in the hope of being nominated to the Senate.

Everything suggests that the National Assembly will sit for the last time on Friday. It will thus come to an end after an existence of nearly five years.

The new parliamentary majority, composed of the Left, the Bonapartists, and a small number of dissidents from the Extreme Right, will vote the immediate termination of the state of siege

The Boulevard de Sébastopol in the Sixties

everywhere in France. The Right and the Centre Right will vote for its maintenance.

M. Buffet's friends are most anxious that he should not make this vote one of confidence.

On the assumption that he keeps his portfolio, M. Buffet has made a deal with a number of Bonapartists whose influence in their own provinces is unchallengeable. He has promised, for instance, not to oppose the candidature of M. Cassagnac junior for the Chamber of Deputies, and that of M. Cassagnac senior for the Senate in the Gers, on the condition that the Bonapartists do not nominate a rival candidate to M. Batbie, the Minister of Education.

Baron Chauraud, the only member of the Extreme Right who has not obtained help from the Left for his election to the Senate, has been nicknamed at Versailles 'The last Christian baron.'

M. Rouher, a former minister of Napoleon III, has gone to Chislehurst to justify himself with the young prince and the Empress Eugénie for his political *volte-face* during the last few weeks.

30th December 1875. The *maréchale* said to her husband at table the other day:

'Maurice, when shall we have a Great Exhibition of Paris?'

'But . . . but . . . I haven't thought about it.'

'You *must* think about it, Maurice.'

'Let me see; we can't have one next year, because of the Philadelphia Exhibition, and the year after that there is one in London . . .'

'Very well,' declared Mme MacMahon. 'We shall have ours in three years' time.'

XIV. THE LAST OF THE LETTERS[1]

18TH *January 1876.* I went through a large number of provincial newspapers this morning, and I noticed that the election of delegates to the Senate is extremely favourable to Conservative opinion in its various forms. Many mayors have been nominated, which is contrary to orders given by the Republican committees. In the Vienne nearly all the mayors are delegates. Two-thirds of those in the Allier are Conservatives. Everything suggests, therefore, that the vote of the delegates on 30th January will produce a strong Conservative majority in the Senate, and such a result might exercise a good influence on the election of deputies. The Republican and Radical newspapers have received instructions to construe even the most Radical elections as successes for the moderate Republicans, leaving themselves free to reveal the true situation later.

Friends of the Orleanist princes have been distributing a brochure of fifteen pages called *La Fortune des Orléans*, published by Santon, 41 rue du Bac, and intended to refute calumnies propagated by the Radical and Bonapartist press.

7th February 1876. It is impossible not to be struck by the language one hears at the election meetings—it is exactly the same as that which preceded the Commune in 1871. The Government would be wise to take precautions. It ought to proceed against speakers who incite to massacres and civil war.

[1] Marshal MacMahon's promise to his wife to hold a Paris exhibition in 1878 was the logical conclusion to this volume. The Republic was confirmed; the National Assembly gave place to a Senate and a Chamber of Deputies. The letters of C. de B. continue spasmodically through 1876 and 1877, and finish altogether in the early spring of 1878, while the workmen were building and painting the exhibition. I have grouped some of these letters into this final chapter.

Otherwise Marshal MacMahon will be called upon to play the role of a Trochu.

Since we hear rumours of war for the spring, I think it my duty to quote from a letter I have received from Prince Jean Ghika in Bucharest, dated 2nd February:

'Here we are arming against—Turkey, I suppose, which is not attacking us. We have bought forty-eight guns, the most modern and efficient that Krupp has made up to date, and we have ninety-six others from preceding years. We are buying 100,000 improved Chassepots. We are going to distribute twelve Grand Cordons of the Order of Charles I, as well as numerous orders of grand officers, commanders, officers, and chevaliers. We are to mint new coins with the effigy of Charles I, and if the Turks are not satisfied we shall refuse the tribute in March, and if, after that, the Turks are still not satisfied, we are going to declare ourselves independent, and if that does not satisfy them, we shall cross the Danube with several hundred thousand Russians. As to what will happen after that, God only knows, unless He has informed Bismarck and Gorchakov, whose agents here appear to be on the best of terms with our agents in Constantinople and St Petersburg, who, after being summoned to Bucharest, went straight back. Tell me if you can see any clearer through this political fog.'

22nd February 1876. The result of the elections so far, and especially the defeat of M. Buffet, have caused much anxiety at the Élysée. The marshal shows ill humour when the question is brought up and immediately changes the conversation. He speaks continually of 'la chasse,' so that it is said of him that he will end by being 'chassé.'

Before replacing M. Buffet and drawing up another ministry, the final results of the elections will have to be considered. These will only be known after 5th March at the earliest. The Bonapartists will have between sixty and sixty-five seats in the new Chamber of Deputies.

Madame Thiers has phlebitis.

The latest election news for the Chamber of Deputies gives 213 Republicans of the Left and the Extreme Left, and to these must be added about seventy who have the most votes in the first ballot, and who would increase the advanced Republican majority to 283.

The Conservatives of all shades (Extreme Right, Right, Centre Right, and Centre Left) have 205 members, to whom must be added about thirty-eight who have the most votes in the first ballot. On certain important questions of social legislation this would give a Conservative minority of 243.

29th February 1876. Since the elections there are both optimists and pessimists in our political and financial worlds.

The optimists believe that there will be a majority in the Chamber of Deputies of 300 against all measures with a Radical flavour. Some Radicals of the late National Assembly, like M. Schérer and M. Kestner, now publicly proclaim themselves Constitutional Republicans. The re-establishment of the National Guard will not be voted. Its chief opponent is M. Jules Favre, who says that during the war the National Guard 'dishonoured itself.'

The request for a general amnesty will be defeated, but the Government will promise to multiply individual pardons.

The pessimists claim that violent elements will be sufficiently numerous to dominate the Chamber and to involve it in grave measures. They claim that the marshal is in the position of Louis XVI with the constitution of 1791, and that he will suffer the same fate. These people also say that the Vicomte Emmanuel d'Harcourt, Secretary of the Presidency, is the 'blind man's dog.'

The Paris carpenters are going on strike unless the employers grant them new conditions of work.

13th March 1876. The general meeting of the senators and deputies yesterday was chiefly interesting for the antagonism shown between M. Jules Simon's friends and those of M. Gambetta. A sensational break is to be expected between these two

Republican parties in the Senate and the Chamber of Deputies. It is known that M. Thiers and M. Jules Simon are hand in glove.

The resolution proposed by M. Gambetta was only passed by some twenty votes. M. Thiers is said to have made the following statement to a number of intimate friends—a statement. that caused enormous interest:

'From now on be careful what you do. The Third Republic is the last which this country will see. Either it will endure or there will be no other, if it does not . . .'[1]

There is a pretty story told about the negotiations between the marshal and M. Périer to form a Cabinet. M. Périer's requests had no limit. He wanted a post of Under-Secretary of State for his son, a place in the Cabinet for his friend X, his relation Z must be Prefect of Police. Finally the marshal asked wearily:

'Monsieur le Sénateur, have you not forgotten to ask something for Madame Périer?'

16th March 1876. The Radical press has talked a lot lately about Mme Massabié, an aunt of M. Gambetta, who has apparently had a stroke at Nice, where she went for the marriage of Mlle Benedetta Gambetta.

When Gambetta, after a family quarrel, came to live in Paris, Mme Massabié followed him. As she had some money of her own, she decided to look after the material needs of the future 'dictator,' thus allowing him to conquer his reputation as a café orator.

Gambetta did not forget Mme Massabié when he became famous. He kept this generous aunt with him, and she continued to rule over his home. Her influence was predominant even in the presence of Mme Laurier, Gambetta's mistress. Until quite recently she guarded the entrance to Gambetta's home like a Cerberus, and it was quite impossible to approach the Demagogue without first interviewing this female, who, if

---

[1] '*Ou elle sera définitive ou il n'y en aura plus d'autre, si elle ne l'est pas* . . .' Marshal Pétain declared the Third Republic at an end in 1940.

she was entirely satisfied with the caller's credentials, would magnanimously accord him an audience after dinner to drink a cup of coffee, adding in her inimitable accent of the Midi:

'Té, my good friend, as you 're a "bon," come for coffee. One cup more or less is no great matter!'

One was thus admitted into Gambetta's intimate coterie, but though Mme Massabié did not grudge the coffee she kept an eagle eye on her nephew's cigars, and the fact that he insisted on having a box of 'Londrès' on the table filled her with fear lest he should offer one to a friend.

30th March 1876. Here is the explanation of the question asked in the Madrid Cortes about the rumours of a successor to M. de Chaudordy.

M. Victor Chauffour, former Republican of 1848, only withdrew his candidature from the eighth ward on 5th March, after the Duc Decazes had promised that Chauffour's nephew, M. Jules Ferry, would be appointed ambassador in Madrid.

But when the Duc Decazes was called upon to keep his promise he answered that, when making it, he forgot that M. Jules Ferry refused to be married in church, and that this made it quite impossible for him to be ambassador in Madrid. He promised to find him another post. But the rumour of the appointment had reached Madrid, and was very badly received; the question in the Cortes followed.

M. Ricard has taken pains to reassure the marshal about the inconveniences of dealing with a Republican personnel whose manners are not always outwardly polished. Some Republican civil servants will be especially chosen for their good manners, and they, only, will be allowed to deal with the president.

To-day at Saint-Roch was celebrated the marriage of Prince Constantine Radziwill, nephew of the German Emperor, and Mlle Blanc, daughter of the farmer-general of the gaming tables at Monaco. This young Radziwill squandered an inheritance of some 500,000 to 600,000 francs in the space of a few weeks in Berlin, and needed another fortune. Invitations were sent out to the highest Parisian society, which, in the main, avoided the ceremony.

6th April 1876. Inquiries have often been made into Bonapartist activities without being able to determine exactly the financial organization of the party. Here are some personal and authentic facts on one angle.

There exists in Paris a federation of shopkeepers, whose headquarters are at 82 Boulevard de Sébastopol. Its organ is the National Union of Commerce and Industry. Outwardly it is a commercial and economic body, with Radical and Socialist, sometimes even Communistic tendencies, though claiming to take no active part in politics. In fact, under the direction of M. Frédéric Lévy and his colleagues, it is a powerful lever for Bonapartist propaganda, especially in electoral matters.

7th April 1876. A diplomatic reshuffle is being prepared at the Ministry of Foreign Affairs. There is talk of sending M. de Chaudordy from Madrid to Constantinople; M. Fournier, recently minister to the Italian Government, would go to Madrid. M. de Saint-Vallier would go to Berlin, though it is said that M. de Bismarck is unwilling to accept as successor to M. de Gontant either M. de Chaudordy, because of the role he played during the war, or M. de Saint-Vallier, because of his intimate friendship with Edwin von Manteuffel.

M. de Corcelle would be recalled from Rome to give satisfaction to the Left. He would be replaced by a mere *chargé d'affaires*. It is doubtful, however, whether the Duc Decazes would take such a decision, which would mean a complete break with the Catholic party.

3rd May 1876. The candidature of M. de Marcère for the Ministry of the Interior is now considered certain in official circles.

The publication of the first number of the newspaper *L'Estafette* has made a real sensation amongst Republicans. Curiously enough, they have not hesitated to hail it as an opposition paper. It is said that the article on the marshal's political views was provided by the secretariat of the Elysée, and was drawn up by MM. d'Harcourt, Buffet, and Dufeuille. M. Dufeuille did the actual writing. *L'Estafette* would be the semi-official paper of the presidency, and M. Daudet is said to have been imposed by the Élysée as editor-in-chief in spite of M. Villemessant.[1]

20th June 1876. Bonapartist circles boast that they have a well organized party ready to act at the psychological moment!

Have you heard the joke that is being passed round in certain Paris *salons*? 'The Prince Imperial is not on the throne because his moustaches are not long enough to hide *ses dents* (Sédan).'

22nd June 1876. Very bitter quarrels within the Bonapartist party. The break between MM. Rouher, Raoul Duval, and Bébric appears to be true. The political clubs even have details about this which I cannot authenticate. Thus it is said that these quarrels are due to M. Rouher's refusal to give 200,000 francs which he promised to M. Raoul David for the creation of an important newspaper. The ex-vice-emperor withdrew his financial offer when the details were almost fixed.

23rd August 1876. M. Gambetta, according to his close friends, is beginning to be anxious about the manifestations of the ultra-Radicals against him. There are to be new meetings insisting on his resignation, and he is receiving anonymous letters threatening him with death if he does not resign. He is accused of violating his promises to the people.

M. Gambetta has asked for police protection. It is the story of Mirabeau and of Danton; revolutions always repeat themselves.

The Prince of Wales arrived in Paris on Monday, and left on Tuesday. Why did he come? Rumour has it that he heard about a singer at the Café des Ambassadeurs in the Champs-Élysées. Having heard her sing, he left the next day.

25th September 1876. M. Thiers arrived in Paris this morning at eight o'clock.

[1] Jean-Hippolyte-Auguste Cartier de Villemessant, famous French journalist (1812–79), who founded the *Figaro*.

Before leaving Geneva he wanted to return to Ferney to see once again the portraits of Voltaire, Frederick, and Catherine II.

On the previous evening he went to visit Mme Tronchin, a member of Geneva's wealthy aristocracy. She is a direct descendant of the celebrated Tronchin, Voltaire's doctor. She showed M. Thiers many letters and manuscripts of the philosopher of Ferney. She refuses every offer to publish these documents.

During his stay in Geneva M. Thiers had M. Jousserandot as his intimate companion.[1]

My friend in Geneva who sends me these details adds that M. Thiers has greatly modified his political views, especially about Russia. He is now certain, because of a conversation with his friend Prince Orloff, that Russia does not want war, but he fears that she is not mistress of her own destiny, and that she is undergoing grave troubles at home from secret societies and Slav conspirators. He believes that the formation of Slav unity will be as fatal to France as was the unity of Germany and Italy. M. Disraeli's latest speech has caused great satisfaction to M. Thiers, because he is convinced that it will bring round public opinion in England—and indeed in Europe.

3rd October 1876. There is a belief in official circles that the party which favours a dissolution of Parliament is becoming stronger, and that the marshal will soon have to make a decision, though many believe that he will lack the necessary energy and initiative.

The Bonapartists, flushed with their recent electoral successes, are in favour of dissolution.

After undermining Belgium, Prussian spies are invading Switzerland.

I learn that the central Government is fully aware of the

---

[1] M. Jousserandot was a professor of Roman law at Geneva. He was sent to Cayenne for a time following Louis-Napoleon's *coup d'état* in December 1851.

activity of these agents, but is quite unable to get rid of them. The Governments of several cantons are openly protecting the German agents, and are showing a keen desire to be annexed by Germany. Many Swiss people also, who have made fortunes by dishonest financial operations, place their hopes in annexation, believing that they could thus earn lucrative posts and honours under a new regime. These facts are given me by a patriotic Swiss, who is very worried. It would be a good thing if our Government realized this.

10th October 1876. I had the honour of acquainting you some days ago of the opinions of M. de Chaudordy, ambassador designate to Constantinople, on the Near East question. M. de Chaudordy admits that nearly all his fellow diplomats fear war, but he says that personally he finds this impossible to believe in. When in 1870 he was delegate to the Ministry of Foreign Affairs he saw certain things which now make it impossible for M. de Bismarck to give Russia *carte blanche* in the Near East. Thus, according to M. de Chaudordy, the St Petersburg Cabinet would never plunge into a war of which Europe would be the theatre without first receiving permission from Berlin.

The Duchess de Persigny, separated from her second husband, M. Lemoinne,[1] who ruined himself in crazy speculation, lives in Paris in the most utter misery.

11th October 1876. News of the acceptation of a six months' armistice by Turkey has produced great satisfaction in political and financial circles. At the Ministry of Foreign Affairs, the sudden friendship between M. Decazes and M. de Chaudordy is causing great interest. What does it mean? Will M. de Chaudordy become the link between the duke, his minister, and M. Gambetta, his hero? Now for a strange rumour. Friends of M. Gambetta say that he is hoping to become vice-president of the Republic during the presidency of the marshal! It is

---

[1] John Émile Lemoinne, French writer and politician, born in London 1815, died in Paris 1892. During the Second Empire he waged a fierce campaign in favour of Liberal ideas.

said that Maître Dubochet, who gave Gambetta such a welcome in Switzerland, has taken charge of the ex-dictator's fortune, which, though carefully hidden, is rumoured to exceed 25,000,000 francs.

M. Gambetta has never admitted the existence of this sum, which is unexplainable. He merely returns 30,000 francs from the Republic, and 10,000 francs which he earns as a deputy. His apartment at the Chaussée d'Antin costs him nothing.

14th October 1876. The feeling in the German colony last evening was that Russia would take no notice of the six months' armistice offered by Turkey. Nevertheless here is the note I received this morning from the Ministry of Foreign Affairs:

'Last night at the Quai d'Orsay a pacific solution of the Near East question was confidently expected.'

I should add that the same feeling is to be found at M. de Rothschild's, who has the name for being infinitely better informed than our diplomats.

In Republican circles there is much talk of a sensational incident, which is expected during the law case brought by Mme de Montijo against several Republican newspapers. The owners of one of these papers, the *Siècle*, is alleged to have documents stolen from the Prefecture of Police in 1870 and 1871 which they intend to produce, and which would cause a terrible scandal.

Radical and Bonapartist newspapers are cutting each other's throats for their respective propaganda. *L'Ordre* already publishes a one-sou paper, *La Voix du Peuple*. Another Bonapartist daily at one sou is about to appear under the old-fashioned title of *Le Petit Caporal*. Its founder and editor is M. Perron, ex-editor of the *Journal Officiel* under the Second Empire.

16th October 1876. The real cause of M. Rouher's recent visit to Arenenberg was, I am assured, the programme of the new Bonapartist party. This question is complicated by the direct intervention during the last few days of the Prince Imperial. A statement was ready which merely involved the new group—

not Napoleon IV personally. This statement had itself been the cause of divided opinion. The older members considered the programme bold, dangerous, and inopportune. The younger members were in favour of its publication. Suddenly it became known that the prince had personally prepared a brochure, almost a book, far bolder than the programme in question. M. Rouher did everything possible to prevent it from being printed, but the prince took no notice. It was at this moment that the vice-emperor [M. Rouher] decided to go to Arenenberg.

M. de Chaudordy's hopes of being Under-Secretary of State at the Ministry of Foreign Affairs, for which he had the support of M. Gambetta, have been shattered by two factors:

1. The efforts of M. Thiers, who does not forgive him for his diplomatic role in 1870.

2. Those of M. Jules Ferry and his friends, who accuse him of having been implicated in the [Monarchist] fusion plan of 1873.

17th October 1876. The Bonapartists boast of having the support of thirty French bishops for an imperial restoration, and they cite, amongst others, the name of Monseigneur de la Bouillerie, coadjutor of the archbishopric of Bordeaux. The Cardinal de Bonnechose, during a recent visit to Rome, is said to have revealed this to the pope.

The Duc Decazes said to a lady who came to see him on behalf of the Empress Eugénie:

'Tell Her Majesty that I have no opinion. I serve my country and will serve any Government which assures the prosperity of France.'

There is much speculation amongst Republicans and Bona-partists about the alterations that the Duc d'Aumale is having made at Chantilly. All this suggests that he plans a long stay, and has given rise to wild rumours:

1. That he is planning a restoration.

2. That he is to marry again.

27th October 1876. Senators and deputies are returning to Paris and Versailles. I have spoken to several, and the Conservatives

A Prussian General at the Time of Sadowa

of all shades are much alarmed at the progress of Radicalism in the provinces, and are determined to insist that the Government shall be firmer with the Demagogues. As for foreign policy, both senators and deputies report that the feeling in the provinces is unanimous that France should keep out of European complications.

High officials of the postal service claim that there is no *cabinet noir* [1] since the fall of Thiers in 1873. The only letters any longer to be opened are those intercepted by virtue of judicial instructions. But I would not be too sure!

18th November 1876. I have it on the highest authority that since the complications in the Near East General Berthaut has redoubled his activity. He now claims to have 900,000 men ready to take the field. The work of organization and equipment goes on without a day being wasted.

Germany has discovered the most minute and precise details of the construction of our forts round Paris. The alarm caused by this discovery is all the greater because of the unusual precautions taken to hide this work from prying eyes. As the cementing of each construction was finished it was covered with earth, so that only the contractor and the chief engineer knew the general lay-out. These precautions were of no avail. M. de Bismarck got to know all he wanted. Is this surprising? Not so. It appears simple when one considers the money the German chancellor spends, and the fact that a deputy who was in his pay during the Second Empire *is still a deputy to-day*!

28th November 1876. There was much talk in a certain club yesterday about the results of the examinations for the Staff College [École Militaire Supérieure]. The examining board was very strict, and out of 500 candidates less than eighty were admitted. All those who were the object of special recommendation were refused.

---

[1] The *cabinet noir* was a secret department of the Post Office, where letters were opened and read. First established by Louis XIV, it was revived at various times.

The Bonapartiſt newspaper, the *Salut*, which died at birth, is resuscitated. It will appear on 10th December. M. Rouher has accepted to be patron, and he will have nothing more to do with the *Nation*, which has gone over to M. Raoul Duval. The *Salut* will coſt five centimes; the direċtor is Vernhette, former secretary to M. de la Gueronnière, a prefeċt under the Empire, but the editor-in-chief, M. Clément Duvernois, will write under a pen-name, because of his recent prison sentence for fraud.

23rd December 1876. M. Jules Simon is not unwilling, they say, to accept the glove thrown down to him by M. Gambetta. Each of the rivals believes that he should be leader of the Republican majority. M. Simon thinks that in the ſtruggle he will have on his side the Centre and the Moderate Left, with the exception of some twenty votes. M. Gambetta would have on his side the support of the Bonapartiſts and, if the Right abſtained, the issue might not be clear, as M. Simon believes.

M. Léon Cohn, appointed by M. Jules Simon to the Miniſtry of the Interior, is a close relation to the M. Cohn who is Paris correspondent of the *Neue Freie Presse*—an agent of M. de Bismarck.

9th March 1877. Many Imperialiſts believe that the marshal could be persuaded to attempt a new Monarchiſt fusion. They claim that the marshal is profoundly disguſted with the presidency. He has a personal spite againſt the Empire dating from his defeat at Reischoffen, for which he holds the emperor responsible. He is very anxious therefore to prevent the Conservatives, in their fear of a revolution, from going over to the Empire, and he might be persuaded that his safeſt policy is to bar the road both to the Empire and to a revolution by uniting the partisans of both branches of the house of Bourbon.

I have already pointed out that many Bonapartiſts are impatient with M. Rouher's prudent policy, and attempts have been made to remove him from party leadership. Some papers claim that Prince Napoleon has been exerting his influence. This is not so. M. Rouher remains all-powerful, and has the full confidence of the Prince Imperial. M. Rouher presides over the committee which directs the Bonapartist newspapers *L'Ordre* and the *Nation*. The *Salut* ceases publication to-day, and will be incorporated with the *Nation*.

23rd March 1877. The anger of the ministerial newspapers just now, their threats and their attempts at intimidation, are merely a cloak for the bewilderment and fear in official circles. These people have lost their heads. No longer even relying on intrigue, with which they normally replace politics, they count how many days they can remain in office. Some try to fill their pockets like servants under notice; others declare that before leaving they will do as much harm as possible.

The Paris garrison is said to be insignificant. The posts within the city have been reduced in numbers and manned by non-commissioned officers. The excuse is that the troops are in the new forts.

26th March 1877. I had the opportunity yesterday of visiting the extreme eastern limit of our new fortifications of Paris— notably the fort of Vaujours, and the gunpowder factory of Sévran just behind.

The fort is excellent. It is badly situated, but that is the fault of the marshal-president, who insisted that it should be advanced to the extreme limit of the hills of Vaujours instead of building it on the escarpment, which would have afforded natural protection. As it is, the fort, which is in the form of an arrow-head, could, in my opinion, easily be captured.

The gunpowder factory is built on modern lines, and strongly reinforced to give adequate protection for the experiments now taking place. New powders are being tried out, and the effects of some are so formidable that the windows at Sévran, Vaujours, and Livry are shaken in spite of the great distance. It is to be hoped that these experiments will give us new explosives to replace the old ones, which proved so inferior to those of the Germans. The President of the Republic often watches the experiments.

3rd May 1877. Friends of M. Voisin, the Prefect of Police, say that there is still a coolness between him and M. Jules Simon. M. Simon asked him for certain concessions in the municipal council.

M. Voisin answered:

'M. le Ministre, in 1870 I was a magistrate at Melun, and the Prussians ordered me to prosecute Frenchmen guilty of too much patriotism. I told them that they could declare me guilty also, but that I would never obey their orders. I was then carried off, a prisoner, to Germany.

'To-day I tell you: "Though you insist on my resignation, which I am ready to give you, I will never sacrifice my conscience to your politics."'

INDEX

229

THE HOUSE OF
ORLEANS

Louis XIII

Louis XIV

Ferdinand-Philippe,
duc d'Orléans
1810–42

Louise
m. in 1832 Leopold I, King of the Belgia

Philippe, comte de Paris (Philippe VII)
1838–94

Robert, duc de Chartres (Robert le For
1840–1910

Philippe, duc d'Orléans (Philippe VIII)
1869–1926
d. without posterity

Jean, duc de Guise (Jean III)
1874–1940

Henri, comte de Paris (Henri VI)
1908–
Present Pretender